Luis

Keep Praying [handwritten]

Mike Hylton [handwritten signature]

He
Intends
Victory

Real-life Stories
of Christians living with AIDS

LUIS
GOD BLESS YOU.
YOU ARE A INSPIRITATION
TO MY LIFE. by
Herbert R. Hall Dan Wooding
JAN 30, 1994

Promise Pubishing Co. Orange, CA, 92665

He Intends Victory
Copyright 1994 by He Intends Victory
Irvine California

Edited by M.B. Steele

Printed in the United States of America

Scripture is from The Holy Bible, King James Version.

L:ibrary of Congress Cataloging-in-Publication Data

Wooding, Dan
       He Intends Victory

ISBN 0-939497-33-6

Foreword

I have a friend who works in the leper colonies on the border between Thailand and Cambodia. A church has been established there as God has begun to move in the lives of those forsaken people. My friend has put flesh and blood on the gospel of Jesus Christ. He doesn't say, "Let me tell you how Jesus loves you." He says, "Let me show you." I asked him once what he considers to be the greatest change he has seen in the lives of these men and women. Without hesitation, he said, "Now, they can look you in the eyes. God has restored their dignity."

We live today in a generation of excess and abandon. Everything became permissible, and now, all across our country, there are wounded lives behind closed doors. When I was co-host of the 700 Club at the Christian Broadcasting Network, I received a letter from a fifteen-year-old boy. He told me he was gay, that he had had several homosexual lovers, but that he wanted to leave this lifestyle and live in a new way. He had watched a program the previous week and had prayed with me and given his life to Christ. I said on the show that if you had prayed and surrendered your life to Christ, then tell someone, get involved in a good local church.

The following Sunday, full of joy and excitement over his new life, this young man went to a church in his neighborhood and, at the end of the service, he went to talk with the pastor. He shared a little of his story and was told, "There's no room for `fags' in this church."

He was writing to me to say goodbye. What I told him sounded good, but it didn't work in the cold, hard world. There was no address. I could only pray for God to be merciful to this broken boy.

AIDS is a deadly disease that has or will touch many of our lives. How will we respond? Some of the people that you will meet in this book ... or in your life ... are victims of blood transfusions or have partners with a double life. Others have fallen prey to this plague through lifestyle choices.

As a Christian, I believe that the **cause** is irrelevant because the **call** remains the same: Love unconditionally as Christ has loved us.

Will we embrace the "lepers" of our day and see their dignity restored as their broken lives are bound up by the love of Calvary? Who will show them this love - you and me? We can spend the next years hiding away in our comfortable corners talking about the love of God ... or we can follow the example of Pastor Bruce Sonnenberg whom you will meet in this challenging book by Dan Wooding. We can get involved in the lives of those who need to be touched and held. We can let them see how Jesus loves them.

Sheila Walsh

Table of Contents

Acknowledgments

I would like to thank the following for their invaluable help in the preparation of this manuscript:

Donelda Dansby,

Sharon Hylton and

Andrew Wooding, my oldest son.

Shepherd and Anita Smith were generous in sharing information concerning AIDS which they have collected through their organization, Americans for a Sound AIDS/HIV Policy.

Thanks go to Rick Rickards for his enthusiastic work on the cover for the book.

Thank you all from the bottom of my heart.

Dan Wooding

Introduction

Jonathan is eight. He has bright, dark eyes, a brilliant smile ... and AIDS. Infected when eighteen hours old through a blood transfusion, Jonathan has learned to live with his mortality and is looking forward to "seeing Jesus and being made all better". His mother, Sheila, sought support and acceptance from the churches in their Rocky Mountain community, knowing she couldn't continue to handle the stress alone. Three churches responded in the same way, by callously stating, "You may come to church, if you leave your son at home."

Hurt by rejection and unable to deal with the daily demands of AIDS, Sheila and Jonathan found compassion and mercy from others outside the church. As the epidemic expands, support groups for families dealing with AIDS are being formed so these critical needs can be met, but most of them are being organized by non-Christians.

"AIDS is a challenge unlike most others the 20th century American church has faced," says a document called, "The Church's Response to the Challenge of AIDS/HIV". This book was published by Americans for a Sound AIDS/HIV Policy which is based in Washington, D.C. "Although the problem is enormous and multi-faceted, it grieves us to think that even one brave boy who loves Jesus has been turned away by the church. The tragedy is that there are thousands of Jonathans across the nation whom the church has feared and rejected." The organization went on to state, "In contemporary society, the demands on the local church are great and AIDS is often seen as just one more demand. But experts tell us that by 1994 every person will know at least one individual infected by HIV. That means every church in the United States will ultimately have to address the issue."

A MEETING WITH HERB HALL

The inscription in the brand new Bible said it all. Herb Hall had written, "To Dan Wooding from Herb Hall. He Intends Victory." Herb Hall heard a weekly broadcast I did with Austin Hill on KYMS radio in Santa Ana, California, in which I had explained that my car had been broken into and my Bible had been stolen. Within hours, Herb was at my office in Garden Grove with a new Bible that he "felt led of God" to give to me. As I looked into his sparkling eyes, I was immediately impressed with his caring attitude.

A few months later, that Bible accompanied me to Essen, Germany, where I worked as a writer/broadcaster with Billy Graham for his historic Mission Europe crusade. The veteran crusader for Christ was conducting the most far-reaching mission of his fifty years as an evangelist. Each night, Mr. Graham's sermons were translated into 44 languages and transmitted by eight satellite links to 1,400 venues across Europe in fifty-six countries, including many in the former Soviet Union.

One of the interpreters was from the former Soviet republic of Georgia and expressed his desire to own an English Bible. So, I handed him Herb's Bible and a copy of Herb's incredible testimony which you are about to read. Now, thousands of miles from Herb's home in Southern California, a Georgian Christian is being blessed by Herb's kindness.

Shortly after this, I was introduced to Tamara Lindley Brown, a vivacious young woman from Huntington Beach, California, who exudes the same love for Jesus Christ that Herb does. Yet, like Herb, she suffers from a terrible desease that is claiming the lives of many in America and other countries around the world. This led me to Mike Hylton, who (like the others) is living a victorious life in Christ despite suffering from an extraordinary set of problems that would drive most of us to black despair.

Then, Pastor Bruce Sonnenberg from the Village Church of Irvine came into my life. This loving cleric has set an example of Christ's love that prompted me to write this book which I trust will impact your life as no other book - other than the Bible - has ever done.

AIDS FIRST DISCOVERED

According to Americans for a Sound AIDS/HIV Policy, AIDS was first described in June, 1981 as "an unusual disease that caused primarily young, homosexual men to lose their ability to fight off otherwise common and non-harmful dieseases." GRID (Gay Related Immune Deficiency, as it was first called) soon took the name of Acquired Immune Deficiency Syndrome or AIDS. It was shown to affect anyone who either sexually or through intravenous means was infected by an agent which caused the immune system to be compromised over time.

The causative agent for the AIDS virus was first discovered by Dr. Robert Gallo and Dr. Luc Montagnier, an American and a Frenchman, who called their discoveries HTLV1 and LAV, respectively. Ultimately, the virus became known and is recognized today as the Human Immunodeficiency Virus, or HIV. After the discovery of the virus, a test for detecting its presence was soon developed. By understanding properties of the antibodies the body produces to defend against HIV, scientists were able to establish its presence.

The discoveries of the virus and the tests for its antibodies have allowed us to understand a great deal about the modes of transmission, the progressive nature of infection, and the devastating effect it has on the body.

A WORLDWIDE EPIDEMIC

"Once the discovery of this disease was made in the early 1980s, scientists sought evidence to find where it had originated so we can better understand its transmission characteristics, as well as gaining insight into how to treat it and end its spread," said Americans for a Sound AIDS/HIV Policy. "As information continued to come into the Center for Disease Control in Atlanta, George, it became apparent that the United States was not the only country struggling with this newly discovered disesase. Cases in Europe were soon identified and traced mostly to Central Africa. It is now believed that in all likelihood the HIV virus originated in Africa and has existed there for at least a number of decades."

Because of urbanization and international travel, as well as expanded land and air communication links within developing countries, people infected with the virus had great mobility and were able to spread it not only within their own borders, but from nation to nation, and from continent to continent. The actual location of the virus origin may never be known, and it is an issue that deserves a great deal of speculation. At this point, however, energies may be better expended in dealing with an ever-increasing epidemic of dramatic proportions.

Some first heard of AIDS when movie star, Rock Hudson, died from complications of the disease. Hudson was followed by a string of celebrities like Liberace and Freddy Mercury, lead singer of the British group, Queen, all victims of the terrible disease.

As many in the church stood on the side lines, stars like Elizabeth Taylor and Elton John (devastated by the death of his young friend, Ryan White) took up the cause of AIDS in the media. Symptomatic AIDS is really the final stage of a disease process which begins long before we see people who are physically ill. We now have glimpses of what the HIV epidemic was like prior to our first recognizing symptomatic carriers in 1981 because of blood samples saved for other reasons. The most noteworthy study is what is known as the Hepatitis B Cohort of San Francisco.

In 1978, the public health community enrolled 6,800 homosexual men in San Francisco in a study of the spread of Hepatitis B. They saved the blood serum samples and were later able to go back and examine each of them after an antibody test for the AIDS virus (HIV) had been developed. What they found was quite remarkable. In 1978, three per cent of that cohort was already infected with HIV. It grew to twelve per cent in 1979, and by 1981 when the first AIDS cases had been discovered, 36 per cent of that group were already infected. Today, nearly 80 per cent of the men in that study are HIV positive. While most still show no symptoms, the numbers of people developing AIDS continues to increase.

HIV is a slow-acting virus and those infected may not show symptoms for up to ten years from the time of infection. Consequently, the HIV epidemic today is mostly unseen because individuals who are infected with the virus do not yet have symptoms. Today's HIV infection will ultimately become the AIDS epidemic of the future.

Dan Wooding
ASSIST
P.O. Box 2126
Garden Grove, CA 92642

Herb Hall

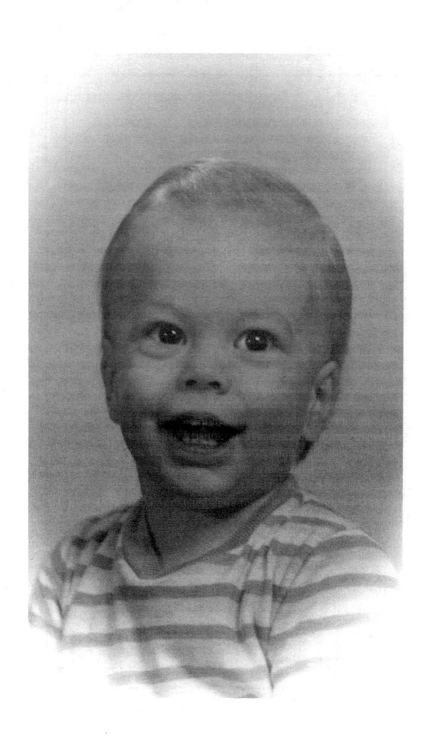

Chapter One

THE WORST OF TIMES

THE DARK SIDE OF THE HALL

Herb Hall's heart was thumping wildly in his chest as he prepared to reveal his terrible secret. What made it so difficult was that Pam, his best friend, looked so lovely as he gazed at her across the table in a restaurant in Garden Grove, California. The terror he felt had multiplied because he was facing what was to be the saddest, yet most courageous moment of his life.

Just a few months earlier, he began to think about proposing marriage to Pam. As far as Herb was concerned, he wanted nothing more than to marry this person he loved more then anyone else in the world. In spite of that, taking a deep breath, he launched into his tragic monologue that would change their lives forever.

"Pam, there is something very, very serious that I have to tell you," he started hesitantly, a mustache of sweat appearing on his upper lip. "There is a dark side of my past that I've never told you about. I've brought you here tonight to tell you about that and also give you some news you must hear." By now the color in his face was high and rising like the morning sun.

Pam shot him a quizzical glance. What on earth was he going to say?

"Herb, let's enjoy dinner first and we can talk about things later," she said.

"No, we've got to talk about it now, because it is very, very, very serious," he persisted.

"Well, let's at least order our food first," she said gently. "Then you can tell me what you have to say." Pam felt she needed to "buy" some time.

"Okay, let's order first," Herb agreed, relieved to have a little more time to gather his whirling thoughts.

IN THE BEGINNING

Herbert Ray Hall was born on April 21, 1956, in the small Midwestern town of Chetopa, Kansas. With a population of just 1,600, it was a long way from the city of Garden Grove in Orange County, Southern California. Garden Grove is the home of Robert Schuller's glittering Crystal Cathedral and his "possibility thinking" theology with a congregation of approximately 120,000 people of just about every nationality ... and Herb Hall. There hadn't been much "possibility" of advancement for Herb, the youngest of six children, in Chetopa. He had four sisters—Judy, Margaret and twin sisters, Jeanne and Janice— and one brother, Mike. The twins were born April 10, 1955, and Herb was born April 21, 1956. "So my mom had three of us within a year and eleven days," he recalled. The winters in Chetopa were long and cold and the summers hot and humid.

Herb's first clash with misfortune took place when he was only two years old. He tripped while running and cracked his head on the corner of a concrete step. This terrible accident blinded him for three days. "They didn't know whether I would ever get my sight back or not, but happily it did return," he recalled. "After that, every time I got hit on the head, I would black out, get nauseated and lose my vision. It always made me really sick."

Consequently, as a child, Herb led a sheltered life. "I couldn't play sports," he said. "I couldn't do many things that my friends did. We went to a little Southern Baptist church there in Chetopa—the First Baptist Church."

"Mom was a devoted Christian," he continued. "Dad was a backslidden Christian and didn't go to church. I really didn't want to go, but because of my mother, I went to Sunday School. When I was seven years old, I gave my life to Christ during an altar call given by the pastor." His relationship with Jesus Christ was a deep comfort to this confused child. The Savior was a true friend who did not reject him, like so many of the school kids.

Because of his continuing illness, Herb's parents took him to the Kansas City Medical Center when he was ten years old. There, extensive tests were carried out and the doctors discovered that he had brain scar tissue from the initial accident. The doctors told Herb's parents that he probably would not have the mental capacity to make it through high school because of this brain damage.

Being a sick, puny kid, Herb continued to feel like "odd man out" in the school activities where being a sports hulk was all important. "I was in junior high when I started really noticing girls and wanting to go to dances and do all the things that junior highers do, but I was always turned down by girls," he remembers.

Because of this rejection, Herb found that all of his school friends were guys. "I started having a physical attraction to them. I knew this was wrong and I really struggled with that, but I said to myself, 'Well, I sure can't tell anybody', and for many years, I didn't," he said.

It was while he was a first year student in high school that his parents decided to head west to Southern California. "Dad just couldn't support the family there in that small Kansas town, and Mom was originally from Southern California. All her family was there, so they decided that we would move to Southern California. That was really a culture shock for me," he recalled.

ALL THE LONELY PEOPLE

Suddenly, Herb was thrust from a town of a few thousand people where everyone knew everyone else, into an area of seventeen million anonymous people. Even the freeway system that crisscrossed the Los Angeles basin was like an old drain filled with rust.

"After we moved, I continued my lonely lifestyle except for a few friends I made at our Baptist Church in Garden Grove," he said.

Despite the negative prognosis of the Kansas City medics, Herb graduated from high school on the Dean's List. "I had a 3.0 average all the way through high school, so I really proved the doctors wrong," said Herb. "God had a plan for my life and that was part of it."

After graduation, Herb went on to Golden West College in Huntington Beach where he also did extremely well. After majoring in a course on the administration of justice, he again graduated successfully.

Still, Herb continued to struggle with his homosexual desires; still, he kept his problem to himself. "I didn't do any better communicating with young women in Southern California than I did back in Kansas," he remembers sadly.

Herb's misfortunes continued while he was at Golden West College. "I was involved in a serious car accident," he recalled. Herb was driving home one Sunday afternoon when the streets were full of water. He peered through the windshield as the wipers clicked back and forth, vainly swatting at the steel-gray curtain of rain tumbling out of the angry sky. Herb was in a lefthand turn lane when he happened to glance up. He was confronted with the terrifying sight of an out-of-control semitruck coming right at him. The action was as if it were a freeze-frame in a motion picture and the only thing Herb could remember was screaming out, "God, help me!" The semi came across two lanes of traffic and hit his car head-on, sending Herb careening and skidding out of control into a nearby cement block wall. In the shuddering impact, Herb's head hit the jagged windshield. Pain called for his attention, but it was faint and far away.

He killed the car's engine and sat there for a long moment, his heart hammering in his chest. He shook his throbbing head. Spots danced before his eyes as he tried to take in his close confrontation with death. Besides a nasty head injury, he also suffered back trauma. "I had three witnesses to the accident and every one of them said, 'You should have been killed. We saw the truck coming'. One couple said they were doing about forty miles per hour in their car when the truck passed them like they were standing still. They had said to one another, 'He's going to end up killing somebody.'"

"Another person, who stopped at the light saw the truck coming out of control and ran the stop light to get out of his way, but unfortunately, I didn't see him in time. The fact that I survived the accident really showed me that God had some meaning for my life."

Despite this setback, Herb went on to California State University in Fullerton where he got his bachelor's degree in criminal justice.

Still wrestling with his homosexual desires, Herb secured a part-time job with Sears as a security officer. "I also had other jobs and all during this time, I remained straight," said Herb. "I am sure that my colleagues didn't suspect the turmoil going on in my heart. After all, I didn't act in an effeminate way, or anything like that. I was really just behaving like any ordinary person. I am sure that none of my family or friends had any clue of the sexual desires I was struggling with."

HERB'S FIRST ENCOUNTER

At the age of twenty-one, Herb finally succumbed to his desires. "I went into a Garden Grove 'adult' bookstore and I got involved in pornography," he recalled sadly. "I watched some homosexual movies and as I walked out of the place, a guy approached me and made a pass at me. That was really all I needed, and so I had my first homosexual encounter that night."

Conscience-stricken, Herb went home. As a Christian, he knew what he had just done was wrong. "I felt really dirty and my heart was completely broken. In the privacy of my bedroom, I prayed, 'God, I'll never do this again. Please help me to get over this,'" he said. "At the same time, I said to myself, 'Hey, if I tell my family, friends and the people at the church, they are not going to have anything to do with me.'" I was really afraid that my church would kick me out, and I told myself, 'I'll have the strength never to do this again.'"

It didn't work out the way Herb had hoped. For the next ten years, he felt an overwhelming compulsion to keep returning to the adult bookstores that dotted that section of Garden Grove Boulevard. "I got deeply involved in more pornography. Every time I went to one of these adult bookstores, I would meet somebody and I'd have a different sexual encounter each time."

"I would get into a car with him and we would drive to a neighborhood park and do sexual acts and stuff. A couple of times I went to the guy's house, but that was sporadic."

Herb's sexual partners were usually anonymous. "I didn't know these men and, usually, they were just one-time sex affairs. After about nine years of this, I was with one man who asked, 'Have you ever heard of the bath houses?' I said that I hadn't, and he said, 'Well, there is this bath house in Long Beach. If you'll drive me down there, I'll show you where it is.'"

"We drove there and I discovered it was a place where men go to have multiple sex partners. I paid the ten-dollar entrance fee and they gave me a membership card. Then you handed over eight or nine dollars each time you went back. They showed homosexual movies and had side rooms where people could go. I still can hardly believe that I got involved in something like that, still, I went to this place for about six months. Each time—afterwards—I felt really dirty."

Herb found that his double life of trying to be a Christian and then performing unnatural sex acts with men, was tearing him apart.

"I had been in that life for about ten years and desperately wanted to break free," he recalled. "Anybody close to me still had no clue about my dark secret. My family, friends, and church thought I was 'straight as an arrow'. They were not aware that I was living a double life."

Because Herb was such an accomplished actor, nobody ever challenged him. "When I wasn't working, I went to church every Sunday," he said. "I also went out with my straight friends from church most Saturday nights. We'd go to the movies and then afterwards, get something to eat. I had four or five really close friends, and they never had a clue of what I was doing. They never knew that I was struggling with homosexuality. To them, I was 'straight' and since I worked security jobs, I appeared to be macho. I think it was my friends that really kept me going. If it hadn't been for them, I think I would have ended my life."

After a decade of living his double life, Herb found he couldn't cope anymore. "I was under a lot of stress at work as a security manager for Sears," he said.

In sheer desperation, he cried out to God, saying, "Lord, I can't live this way anymore. I don't want to be homosexual, and if my friends or family or church discover my secret, I'm dead! I'm going to take my life."

Herb went home from his job one bleak Saturday morning determined that suicide was the only solution to his agony. His doctor had prescribed "a whole bunch of pills" for depression and his constant headaches. In his bedroom at home, his eyes blinded by tears, he picked up a pen and wrote out a quick note to whomever would discover his lifeless body.

With trembling hands, he scribbled, "My life isn't worth living," and then downed a complete bottle of pills. With that he lay on his bed at his parents' home and waited for death to come and blot out the ceaseless pain.

As he began to slip into eternity, he heard the incessant ringing of the telephone in the kitchen. It turned out to be his former boss at Sears who had been concerned about Herb's depression ever since he had worked there.

"She was a Christian, and she knew that I was really going through tormenting times and struggling with my job, though she didn't know about my homosexuality," said Herb. "My mom answered the phone and I vaguely heard her say, 'He's not feeling very well. He's in bed, but I'll see if he wants to talk to you.'"

Unaware of the life-and-death drama being played out behind the wall a few yards away, Mrs. Hall knocked at the bedroom door and said, "Herb, Nancy's on the phone, would you like to talk to her?" Since he didn't answer, she entered the room. Suddenly, her eyes got as big as saucers as they fixed on the empty pill bottle and the suicide note.

She ran out of the room, told Nancy what she had discovered, and quickly called the paramedics. The dedicated men were soon on the scene and began working feverishly on Herb. They induced vomiting and then rushed him to a nearby hospital.

"I was admitted as 'fifty-one-fifty,' the welfare institute's code that said that I was a danger to myself," said Herb. "They put a seventy-two-hour psychiatric hold on me."

"GOD CAN DELIVER YOU"

One of his first visitors was Tony Britton, pastor of his church. As he sat and gazed at Herb's ashen face, he said, "Herb, I don't know what you're struggling with. I don't know what your hurts are. I don't know what your pain is. But I do know that God loves you, and He can forgive you of anything that you've ever done. He can deliver you from the hurts you've been carrying."

For the first time since beginning his double life ten years before, Herb began to open up. "I told him about my homosexuality," recalled Herb.

Herb was surprised with the pastor's understanding tone. "Well, Herb," he said gently, "you know, we can get you help, and we will pray for you because God can deliver you from this problem. God can really help you and change your life for good."

Tony Britton did pray with him that God would deliver him from his homosexuality. Herb also summoned up the courage to tell one other friend.

"After I was discharged from the hospital, I went through counseling for three years and God completely changed my life," said Herb, his face now alight with joy. "During those three years, I was completely delivered from the homosexual lifestyle."

LOVE AT FIRST SIGHT

For the first time in a decade, Herb Hall began to feel optimistic about his life. Then came an added bonus.

"I fell in love with Pam, this wonderful woman at our church," he said. "After a year, I knew that I loved her so much I vowed that someday I would marry her."

By this time, AIDS had been on the scene for a while, and so Herb was aware that he should be tested before he got married. Still, it held no terrors for him. He said to himself, "Hey, I'm a Christian. There is no way that I can have AIDS."

In October of 1989, he went to the Orange County Health Department in Santa Ana, California, and underwent the HIV test.

"There was a two-week waiting period after your blood was drawn, then you went back and they told you whether you tested positive or negative. A week had passed since the test and I was working in security for McDonnell-Douglas in Long Beach, California. One day, I got really sick and collapsed on the job."

"I was unconscious when they rushed me to the hospital and when I came to, I told the doctor that I had taken an HIV test. He said, 'What were the results?' I said I didn't know—I hadn't gotten them back yet. His response was, 'Well, your blood work is really looking good' so he gave me a sense of hope that I wasn't HIV positive and this collapse was due to other causes."

THE TEST RESULTS

After being released from the hospital, Herb got up the courage to return to the Orange County Health Department for the results of his anonymous testing. It was now near the end of October, 1989.

A peculiar foreboding hung over him as his mother drove him there and nothing could alleviate this strange nervousness. "We stopped in front of the Health Department and prayed together as we sat in the car," Herb recalled. "I then went in to get the results.

For some reason, I knew in my heart that the test was going to be positive, even though I tried to deny that terrible feeling."

The closer he got to the clinic, the more nervous he became. Herb gave the nurse his number and she said, "Okay, we're going to take you into this room, and somebody will soon be in to go over your test results with you."

His heart was pounding unmercifully as he sat waiting in the room for about five minutes. Then the door opened and a nurse entered clasping his file.

"Mr. Hall," she began, after clearing her throat, "I'm sorry to tell you that your test came out positive."

Herb's heart sank on hearing this death sentence—HIV positive! The words echoed painfully in his mind. He found himself frozen in his chair, gripping the sides with white knuckles. The swiftness with which his world dissolved was like a black pool of murk engulfing him. He did not want to look into it for fear he would see things he did not want to remember.

Tears stung his eyes and his face flushed crimson. "I didn't know what to say," he recalled. "I managed to silently stumble out my response. 'God, this isn't fair. I've given my life back to You. I'm serving You. I've left that lifestyle—and now this!'"

What also hit Herb at that moment was that his family and most of his friends from the church didn't know anything about his past life. What was he going to do?

"I knew I would have to tell everybody that not only had I been in a homosexual lifestyle, but that now I had AIDS," he said. "My mind became a blur." Herb was swamped with an overwhelming sense of futility and loneliness.

The nurse said, "I want to give you a packet of information. It tells you about support groups. It also tells you where to go for medical treatment."

Unable to comprehend the news, Herb shouted at the nurse, "The test is wrong! I want you to take it over again!"

Understanding his anguish, the woman explained the procedure that was used to test the blood. "They sent it through several other tests that came up positive. The tests are 99 percent accurate. There is no way that we could have made a mistake with the tests. I'm really sorry, sir, but we know that you are positive."

To add to the humiliation of the moment, the nurse asked him, "Could you provide us with a list of everybody that you've been with so that they can be notified that you've tested HIV positive?"

Herb responded that he couldn't because "most of them were just one-time, anonymous encounters."

His legs felt rubbery and his palms were sweaty. Herb stumbled past the crowds of people at the health center and headed toward the car where his mother was waiting in anxious silence. Tears blinded his eyes as he climbed in and told her bleakly as the blood drained out of his face, "I've tested positive." His mother—whose face was pale—began to cry and between their heartfelt sobs, they both prayed that God would somehow bring good from this terrible predicament.

Herb set up an appointment with his personal doctor to have further blood tests done. "We're going to draw your blood, and check your T-cells," he told Herb.

At the time, Herb didn't know anything about AIDS or what T-cells were. "My doctor explained that T-cells are our immune system," said Herb. "He said they're what fight viruses and germs that come into our body. When I went back about two weeks later to get the test results, the doctor told me, 'Herb, your T-cell count is only 170. An average person has 1,200 to 1,500 T-cells. You've only got about 170 T-cells left. You're probably only going to live one more year.'"

It seemed to Herb that terrible news was never-ending. Only one year left to live! "This was back in 1989, so we've come a long way since then," he said. "But in 1989, this MD really didn't know a lot about AIDS." Still, Herb Hall faced an intolerable web of circumstance.

THE PRODIGAL RETURNS

This latest setback made Herb decide that in whatever time he had left on this earth, he would never again be a phony. "I immediately went home and told all my family," he said. "I gathered my parents and brother and sisters together and shared my terrible news with them."

He stated, "I'd lived that lifestyle for ten years. It had been a life of being phony in everything. I'm not going to live anymore being phony. I'm going to tell people where I've been and what I've done and that I have AIDS."

One by one, his family stood and hugged him. The unlikely prodigal had returned to the fold!

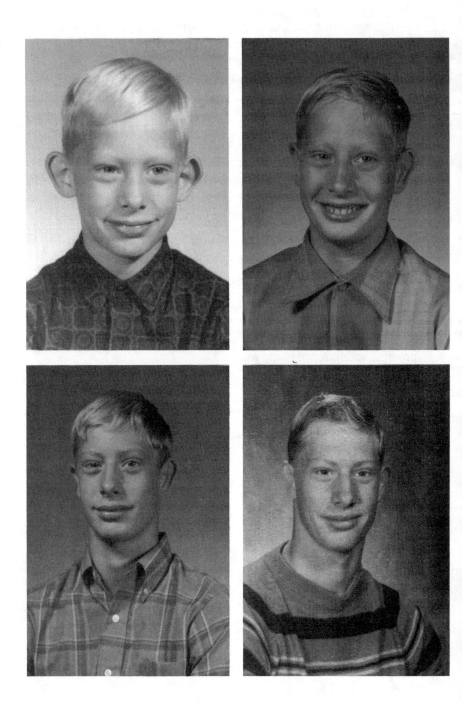

Chapter Two

THE BEST OF TIMES

Herb thought his heart would break as he finally was ready to tell Pamhis terrible news. They ordered their food and she sat quietly, awaiting his impending news.

"Okay, Herb, tell me what you have to say," she said, sipping from the glass of ice water. "I'm all ears, as they say."

Herb took a large gulp of air, pushed his hair back with a nervous hand, and then began—his face flushed with pain. "Pam, as I have already said, there has been a dark side about me that you nor anyone else knew about."

There was a long, awkward silence from both of them, but Herb pressed on, his voice barely audible over the noise of the restaurant. "You never knew that for ten years I led a double life," he said. "I became hooked on homosexual pornography and eventually got involved in that lifestyle. I went out with a number of men whom I met outside adult bookstores."

"I continued going to church, but this problem overwhelmed me and I was very weak-willed. Then, three years ago, I re-committed my life to Jesus Christ and came out of living that lie. God delivered me completely and, as you know, I fell in love with you. You are the most wonderful person I have ever met. I love you more than you will ever know."

By now, Pam's eyes had paled like white diamonds, but she didn't speak.

"The worst part of this is that I have tested positively for AIDS. I went to get tested so I could ask you to marry me. Now we can't get married or have children," he said, his voice cracking hoarsely with emotion. Herb clasped his hands on the table and stared down at them.

Pam looked at Herb with stricken eyes and began to sob quietly, but after a couple of minutes, she was able to compose herself. She wasn't feeling sorry for herself, but for her dear, dear, friend.

She marshalled her strength and then wiped the tears from her face with a small, crumpled handkerchief. Finally, she told him in a hushed voice as her lower lip quivered with emotion, "Herb, you know I care about you no matter where you've been or what you've done. You will always be my friend. I will always be there for you. You can count me to stick by you."

For Herb Hall, these were the sweetest words he had ever heard. He reached across the table and gently touched her hand.

And Pam was true to her word. "She has been my friend since then for almost four years," said Herb. "Every Saturday night, we go out to the movies, and then get something to eat."

"She calls me two or three times a week and asks me how I'm feeling. She has been my closest friend."

A STEP FURTHER

After the get-together with Pam, Herb decided to take his honesty one excruciating step further. He went to see Tony Britton at the Baptist church. "Tony, I want to go public with what has happened to me," he told the pastor. "I want to tell the whole church." The pastor was all for it.

"So he called all the deacons and everybody together and we set up a Sunday night meeting so that I could share my story," said Herb. "Before that I met separately with about ten of my best friends and told them my news in advance. Each of them was sympathetic and reached out to me. They really showed me love and compassion. Naturally, they were shocked. They hadn't had a clue as to what had been going on in my life."

"So, that Sunday night, I went before the church. I told the whole congregation about the life that I had been living, and how God had changed my life. I explained that I had been out of 'the life' for three years and now that I had been sick, I had been tested for AIDS. I was positive."

One person got up and walked out of the church. "You know, he just couldn't handle it and he never came back. Everyone else was supportive," Herb said. "Many people came to me afterwards. They were crying and they hugged me."

Despite the support he was receiving, Herb began to feel a dragging sense of bewildered desolation concerning this situation which he could not understand. He began searching for Christian support groups for people who were HIV positive, but in 1989, there were none to be found. The only ones functioning were for homosexuals with AIDS, and he was unwilling to attend one of those because he knew that he had been delivered from that lifestyle. He didn't want to be back in that environment.

"I've been clean for three years, and I don't want to go back to that type of life," he prayed.

"So I struggled with what to do. For a year, my friends really helped me get through, but I was depressed most of the time," he recalled. "I was really moody, then after a year, my life again started falling apart."

To add to his woes, he began to believe he would be laid off from his job as a security officer at a large aircraft company in Long Beach due to cuts in the aerospace industry. "I also began to feel that my friends didn't want me around them anymore," he said. "I wasn't being invited to the activities that I used to attend anymore, and several of my friends got married."

"I could not realize at the time that their lives were changing—they were getting married and starting families. I just thought, *'Hey, because of this disease, they don't want me to be around any more. They're not inviting me to parties and other functions because I have AIDS. They just don't want me to be there.'*"

"I couldn't see that their lives were changing and now they were settling down to have families. I just figured that they hated me. I became disconnected from those I loved and I fell into a mood of bleak despair."

His colleagues at the aircraft company were unaware that he had AIDS, but they suspected he had a terminal illness after he had been admitted to the hospital and was away from the job for several weeks. "Before the lay off, they really reached out to me," he said. "They gave me a position in the company where I could continue working and handle the responsibility. They were really super to me."

The day the ax fell, his boss called him at his post in the parking lot and said, "Herb, we're sending a car over to pick you up. We're relieving you of your duties. I want to talk to you."

Fearing the worst, Herb was driven over to his office. "Herb, I've heard some rumors that you're really sick and you have a terminal illness, and legally, you know, I really can't ask you what your illness is," said his boss, folding his arms across his chest.

Herb remained silent.

"You have been a really good worker here. People really like you," he continued. But is it true that you are seriously ill?"

"Yes," was all he could stiffly stammer out.

"Well, I just want to tell you that this company will do everything possible to help you to continue to work," he stated.

Relieved that he still had a job, he muttered a heartfelt, "Thank you," to his boss.

He was then driven back to where he was working, but about an hour later, the phone rang again. It was the same man. "We're sending another car over to pick you up," he said on the phone.

Herb's heart skipped a beat. He thought, "*Oh no, this is it. They're going to get rid of me now.*"

He returned to his boss' office where he explained, "After you told me that you were really sick, I called the union steward and I also called the chief. They came to my office and we told them about your problem. I see here that you have a request for weekends off." Herb had asked for Sundays off so he could go to church, but it was about a year-and-a-half wait to get weekends off because they had to go by seniority.

"There is a special thing in our union contract that if a person's ill and the union agrees and the company agrees, we can give you a special position to help you out," he pressed on. "We're willing to do that. I also see you had a request for weekends off so you can go to church, and I think that is really needed."

"Starting this weekend, you'll have weekends off. You'll work the day shift—you know, Monday through Friday, and we will put you in the lobby."

Another reprieve. Again, he breathed a sigh of relief. "They made the job really easy for me," said Herb.

The man couldn't have been more understanding. "Herb," he concluded, "I'm very sorry that this had to happen because you've been a great worker—especially facing, you know, a terminal illness, but we have no choice. We have to go by what the union says."

It was another year before Herb again got to the point where he was about to be laid off. The news in the press wasn't good. The

"Peace Dividend" with the former Soviet Union meant that the defense industry would suffer, and the lay off would become inevitable.

THE APPROACHING AX

As the ax approached—and with the feeling that his friends had turned their back on him, Herb began to believe that the only way out was to take his own life.

"I felt my friends didn't love me anymore," he said bleakly. "It seemed to me that they didn't want me around, so I was really down."

At this low ebb, feeling a weariness heavy within himself, Herb decided to end it all with a gunshot to the head. He vowed, "Today I will take my life. My life is no longer worth living."

He explained, "I carried a gun at my job and so I knew that I had the weapon to finish it all."

Herb lived in Corona, California at the time, about thirty minutes away from where he worked.

"When I drove home on the Riverside Freeway that day—it was Memorial Day weekend of 1990—I vowed that I would kill myself," he said. "At this point, all my close friends were going camping—a couple of them were married and this other couple was engaged to be married. Well, I wanted to go camping with them so bad. I was really hurting that weekend and indirectly they had made it clear that they didn't want me to go. They didn't invite me although I kept on bringing it up, by saying, 'You know, I'd really like to go.' But evidently they didn't want me around."

What Herb hadn't realized was that it was a couples' weekend, and they didn't really want a single person to attend and then feel left out.

"I really took that to heart and, so I was really hurting. I knew they were getting ready to go, so I drove home from work that day and vowed, 'Today. This is the day I'll end my life.'"

In one desperate plea for love and understanding, he called a young woman from his condo who was in the fellowship. The telephone began ringing at the other end of the line. As she answered, he told her, in a discouraged voice, "Alicia, today I'm going to end my life." With that he hung up. Then he called Judy, his sister and told her the same thing.

"I got out of my condo in Corona because I knew they would call the police and I knew they would show up," he said. "I left my wallet at home so they couldn't identify me when I killed myself. I took just enough money to be able to go to a hotel with my gun," he said.

"I got in my car and I was driving on the freeway. For the first time in my life, I felt that God spoke to me in a verbal way," he recalled. "It was as if the Lord said to me, 'Herb, when are you going to give your life to Me 100 percent? When are you going to trust Me for what I'm going to do in your life?' I'd never heard the Lord speak to me that way before."

He drove off the "57" freeway at the Katella Avenue exit in the city of Anaheim and stopped at an ARCO station where there were two pay phones. "I again called my sister and said, 'You know, Judy, I'm going to go check myself into the psychiatric ward of a hospital.'"

Judy responded, by asking, "Herb, where are you? I want to come get you."

"No," he said insistently, "I'll just drive myself there." Then he asked Judy to call Alicia and give her the telephone number where he was and ask her to call him.

Alicia never called. As he anxiously waited, a man pulled up to use the telephone, and he started to pick up the same phone that he was waiting for the call on.

"Excuse me, could you please use the other phone, I'm waiting for a call," Herb said with tears in his eyes. He turned around to Herb, and said, "No problem." Then he saw the tears streaming from Herb's pained eyes. "There's something wrong with you, isn't there?" he suggested.

"Yes," Herb stammered in an almost hypnotic state.

"Well, you know, I'm a Christian and I work at a Christian radio station," he said in a deep, sonorous voice that suggested he was a broadcaster. To Herb, in his hour of need, God sent an angel to take care of him.

"He stayed with me and prayed and talked with me until my sister arrived," said Herb. "This man gave me his card and I ended up losing it. I never saw him again. I don't know if he was an angel—whether he was real or not, but I do know that God sent someone there to help me."

Herb spent a week in the hospital where God began to deal with him. "I got out of the hospital and Pam called me and said, 'Herb, I was listening to KYMS (a local Christian radio station in Anaheim) and I heard this pastor talk about a brand new HIV/AIDS support group that they are going to start at his church—the Village Church in Irvine.'"

Pam gave Herb the telephone number and he called it on Monday morning only to discover that the office was closed that day.

"My heart sank," Herb recalled. "So then I called Tuesday and got a hold of the pastor. His name is Bruce Sonnenberg, and Bruce said, 'Yeah, we're having our first group meeting Thursday night.' I went, and there were three other people on that Thursday. I was touched that night. I remember asking Bruce as I got ready to leave, 'Bruce, how come you would start a support group like this?' Bruce proceeded to tell me about a family that attended a church.

"A husband and a wife had a son that they found out was homosexual and had AIDS and their son's friend went to a different church in a different area. When the son told the church that he had AIDS, the pastor said, 'You're not welcome here anymore.' So Bruce's heart was touched and he went back to his congregation and said, 'Jesus always reached out to the least, the last, and the lost, and we will always be a church that reaches out like Jesus did. We will reach out to people with HIV and AIDS, and if you agree with me, will you stand?' Bruce said that time seemed to stand still as he waited for their response.

"The whole congregation stood, and at that time Bruce said the Lord put it on his heart to start an HIV/AIDS support group to reach out to people. At that time, Bruce was on the board of directors with the Orange County Rescue Mission and there were two or three people staying at the mission that were HIV positive. Bruce knew them, so he really had a heart to reach out to people with HIV and AIDS. I continued going to that support group.

"When I went in the room that first time and met Bruce, it was like I had known him all of my life. He had one of the greatest personalities! He was so loving and so caring, it was just incredible. I had really never ever met a pastor like that, and the first thing that went through my mind was, 'Hey, churches and pastors don't want to do anything with people with AIDS because they are so fearful—people are afraid they can contract AIDS by casual contact—by hugging somebody, you know, being in the same room, and I expected Bruce to be that like that. He was the total opposite.

"Bruce wasn't afraid. He wasn't afraid being in the room with us knowing that we had AIDS. So anyway, we went around the room that night and everybody gave their name and shared, and we all shared how we contracted the disease. It was very interesting because I was the only person in the room that had contracted it through homosexual contact. The other people in the room had contracted it by drug use. So it was a kind of feeling that, you know, although everybody had the disease and drug addicts got it a different way, it was almost like I felt like everybody else in the room would hate me because I had been homosexual. But that really wasn't the case. It was a neat time that night of finding out how other people got the disease and that we were all Christians and that we loved the Lord. It was through that meeting that we started to meet every week at the Village Church."

For Herb Hall, the years of exile were over. He was free at last!

Chapter Three

TICKING TIME BOMBS

"I'm sorry to tell you," said Bruce in his soft Californian accent, "that George passed away last night." The tightly-knit, HIV-positive group at the church looked sad with the report. "But, guys, remember the good news that he is now with the Lord. Let's at least rejoice at that."

Wry smiles creased the faces of those there who were all too aware of the ticking time bomb inside their finite bodies. Taking care of each other was the key to the success of this caring HIV-positive group.

Don Smith had founded the Naaman's Fellowship (named after Naaman, the "Gentile" commander in the Old Testament who had leprosy) to be a Christian AIDS ministry in Long Beach reaching out to people with HIV and AIDS. He visited the support group at the Village Church.

Herb continued his narrative with the author,"One day, Don called Bruce and he invited Don to come to one of our meetings," said Herb. "It was then we discovered that, in his earlier years, Don had been addicted to alcohol and prescription drugs. In time, he had given his life to the Lord and went to work at the Union Rescue Mission in Los Angeles."

"They helped him with his addictions, and Don ended up washing dishes and generally helping out at the mission. Eventually, he was appointed to the board of directors for the Union Rescue Mission. He stayed with them for ten years."

During that period, Don had seen many people with AIDS dying on the streets. Then, to further bring home the horror of the disease, he had a really good friend, an addict who had been diagnosed with AIDS even though he had been clean and sober for a couple of years.

"So, Don watched helplessly as one after another died a terrible death. He took the vision back to the mission and said, 'We need to do something. These people are dying with AIDS and they have no place to go.'"

So, the Union Rescue Mission gave Don Smith a grant and he initiated the Naaman's Fellowship. Herb became a part of that outreach and was on their board of directors for two years. Besides providing accommodations, the fellowship also advised churches that didn't know what to do with HIV-positive people in their congregations.

HE INTENDS VICTORY

Herb was grateful to still be alive despite the doctor's prognosis and now he wanted to get even more involved with others suffering from this desolate disease.

One day, he was having a conversation with Bruce Sonnenberg in his study. "You know, Bruce, there are no other Christian support groups for HIV-positive people in Orange County," said Herb. "I really believe we should start a non-profit organization to help people with this problem."

Herb continued his interview with the author, "God had worked in my life, and what was really neat is that over that year (after I went through the severe depression and saw I was not going to die), I made a wonderful group of new friends," he said.

"I really love my old friends, but I had kept my eyes focused on them. I had all my hope in my friends and I was afraid of losing them. I really believe to this day that God knew what was happening. I now know that He doesn't take something away from you that He doesn't replace with something better."

ONE DAY AT A TIME

"I now have more friends than I ever had in my life, and God has placed many great people in my life. He has changed me and today I live one day at a time."

"I think of my good friend Barbara Johnson of 'Spatula Ministries' who had a homosexual son. They were estranged for many years and she started this ministry to help parents that struggle with having children who are homosexuals."

Herb likes to quote Barbara Johnson who has said, "Yesterday is a canceled check, tomorrow is a promissory note, but **today is cash**."

He stated, "I'm happier now than I've ever been in my life. People don't understand that. They ask, 'Herb, how can you be so happy knowing that you have AIDS; that you may die real soon?' I respond by saying, 'Because I'm a winner any way that I go. If I die today, I'm going to be with the Lord and I'll have a brand new body. If God leaves me here, I'll be able to continue sharing the Gospel and sharing His love with other people.'"

"So, today, I'm living in the best days of my life! I wouldn't change it for anything because of the walk that I have with the Lord."

THE TIME IS NOW

Herb was beginning to feel that it was time to change churches; however, it was a big decision for him since he had been attending the Baptist church for about twenty-three years.

"I had prayed about leaving my church and going to the Village Church of Irvine and, for a year, God appeared to shut that door. I pray that during my last year at the Baptist Church, I touched somebody's life. There were many loving people at my church that really loved and supported me."

After a lot of prayer, Herb spoke with Bruce Sonnenberg about what was on his heart. "Bruce, my present church does not seem to have the vision to reach out to people with HIV and AIDS, and I really want to see this ministry expand," he said. So he asked Bruce to pray "that God's will be done."

Bruce said without hesitation, "Herb, I spoke to the elders about you just last night." He had shared with them about the vision to start a then nameless ministry to the rejected AIDS community.

"The elders want me to tell you that they support you one hundred percent, and that they're willing to let the ministry use office space here at the Village Church of Irvine," he continued. "They're also willing to let us use the phones, the photocopying machine, and the computers. The church secretary, Barbara Haddad, can answer the phone for this new ministry."

These heartening comments were confirmation from the Lord about the move. Herb felt it was time to move his church home as well. "Bruce," said Herb, with tears welling up in his eyes, "I want to be a part of a church that is supporting our ministry and doing what this church is doing." Bruce reached over and hugged Herb and Herb knew that he had finally COME HOME!

So he left the Baptist church after twenty-three years and went over to the Village Church of Irvine. He was warmly accepted by the congregation.

"It is incredible the way this church reached out and loved me," said Herb.

He said that his last day at the Baptist Church was tinged with sadness for him. "The pastor announced on that last Sunday morning that I was leaving to go to another church to start a new ministry," said Herb. "Several members who had supported me all along in the ministry told me, 'Herb, we will continue to pray for you and support you.'"

The He Intends Victory ministry was finally launched in September of 1992. Herb had been "wracking his brain" for a name for the ministry.

"I have a good friend named Mike Hylton who's a hemophiliac. He and a friend were the ones who came up with the name He Intends Victory for HIV," recalled Herb.

"Mike is a devout Christian," added Herb. "He has a lovely wife and three children. Mike blesses my heart and touches my heart because he got the HIV virus through the blood supply. Mike did nothing immoral or anything like that to get the disease. If anybody should be angry it should be Mike, especially since he has three teenage kids and a wife, but Mike loves the Lord and he says, 'I know God's got a plan to do something special with my life through all of this.'" We asked Mike to be on our board.

"I have another friend, Tamara Lindley Brown, a really neat, HIV-infected Christian woman. Her two-year-old son and her husband are both HIV-negative. She also joined our board. Another church member, Mike McIntyre, at the Village Church shared the vision. Mike is now the treasurer."

"So we have five board members at He Intends Victory; three of us are HIV positive. We know Tim Berends with KBRT (a Christian radio station in Southern California) who really has a heart to reach out to all people around the world. We prayed about it and asked him to join our board." The author counts it a privilege to be on the Board also.

The ministry sees its three-part vision as:

1) To reach out to people with HIV and AIDS.

Some don't know Jesus Christ and are heading at breakneck speed into a Christless eternity. We also want to reach out to Christians who discover they have the AIDS virus. "This," says Herb, "is an opportunity for the church to act. We bring a strong message to the church that AIDS is not a plague—it's an opportunity. That is our number-one focus—to share the Gospel with **the least, the last, and the lost** the way Christ did when He was on earth."

2) To reach out to the church.

"Most churches today," said Herb, "have turned their back on people with HIV and AIDS, but not because they don't care. It's because of the fear factor. We really believe that if we can educate the churches to the fact that the virus is not casually transmitted and they don't have to fear the individual, then we can help the church set up AIDS policies. That way, they'll be able to handle it when they find someone who is HIV positive in their church. That way, they'll be able to do what God really wants them to do."

3) The third part is to go into the hospitals, the hospices and the community and reach out to people with the disease.

"In one year, I saw ten people with AIDS give their lives to Jesus Christ before they died. They are now with the Lord."

Chapter Four

THE LEAST, THE LAST,
AND THE LOST

Herb Hall certainly practices what he preaches. He spends hours each week visiting dying AIDS patients. He says the saddest part of his ministry is "seeing people die without accepting Jesus Christ as their personal Savior." But, he has also witnessed to many others, urging them to make that life-changing commitment, some within hours or days of passing away.

Herb recalls one phone call from a lady who told him, "My friend, Mike, is dying of AIDS." She asked if Herb would come see him, so Herb set up an appointment and visited him at an apartment complex where the young man was staying.

"He was in the last stages of AIDS and weighed only about eighty pounds. He looked like a skeleton. When I arrived, the girl who was taking care of him said, 'I'm going to run some errands and I'll be back in about an hour.' When she left, I started telling Mike about my life and testimony and shared the Lord with him."

After about an hour, Herb asked his new friend, "Wouldn't you like to ask Jesus Christ into your life? Wouldn't you like to have a completely new and different life and have peace as well?"

The dying young man looked up at him, tears streaming down his emaciated face, and said, "Herb, I can't."

Herb was confused. "Mike, why not?" he asked.

Mike responded, his voice cracking with emotion, "Herb, three years ago when I was well, a friend shared Jesus with me. I didn't ask Him into my life then. I am sure that God doesn't want me now that I'm sick."

Herb turned to Mike and said, "You know, my friend, when Jesus was crucified, he hung between two thieves. One of them cursed and mocked Him and called Him every name in the book, but the other thief turned his head and said, 'This man has done nothing wrong. We are getting what we deserve. We're criminals. We've killed people, but this man doesn't deserve this punishment.' And he said, 'Jesus, when You come into Your Kingdom, would You remember me?' Jesus turned to that thief and said, 'Today, you will be with Me in paradise.'"

Herb explained to Mike, "If that wasn't a last-second decision, I don't know what was. Jesus loved that thief, Mike, and He loves you today just as much as He loved the thief two thousand years ago on the top of Calvary Hill."

Mike was quietly weeping as he said, "Herb, I would really like to ask Jesus to come into my life right now." With that, Mike reverently bowed his head and began to pray.

"Please, Lord Jesus," he said in a faint, weak voice, "come into my life and forgive me for the terrible things I have done."

A TRANSFORMED LIFE

"For the last two months he lived, Mike's life was completely transformed," recalled Herb. "I was only able to go see him a couple of times after that, but on each occasion, he'd say, 'Herb, I have Jesus in my heart, and I'm at peace!'"

When Mike passed away, Herb asked the girl who had been taking care of him how long she had known Mike. "About a year," she said.

This dedicated woman went on to tell Herb the story of how Mike and she had started a new job at the same time with the same company. "We became good friends and occasionally I'd talk to Mike about the Lord, but he told me he was in the New Age Movement," she said. "He was into crystals and pyramids and everything that goes with New Age thinking."

One day, Mike got really sick and was rushed to the hospital. "I continued to visit him for about two weeks," she recounted. "At first he wouldn't tell me that he had AIDS, but one day Mike opened up and told me the truth. He said, 'I don't want to die in a hospice all alone.'"

Sensing she needed to take immediate action, she talked to Mike's dad, and he agreed to pay for an apartment for him to stay in. So she quit her job and unselfishly took care of Mike for a year.

"If that's not Christianity in action, I don't know what is," Herb said to me soberly.

Mike's caretaker occasionally had the radio in the apartment tuned to a Christian radio station, and Mike listened. "Do you think one of those pastors would come to see me?" he asked her one day after listening to the steady ration of pious preachers.

"Over a period of a year, I called sixteen churches and never got a response from any of them," she told Herb.

When he heard this, Herb was heartbroken. "I know that Jesus would never have failed him like that," said Herb. "He never turned His back on those that needed Him. In fact, just the opposite—He sought them out."

She called the Village Church number and spoke with Herb. After Mike had given his life to Jesus Christ, Mike told her, "Please take all these pyramids and the crystals and throw them in the trash. They don't work." She was glad to report that she was able to comply with his request.

Then, when each of his friends called on the phone, he'd tell them proudly, "I have asked Jesus Christ into my life."

When she opened the shades each morning, Mike would say, "Please sing to me, 'This is the Day That The Lord Has Made,'" which, of course, she did. "His face lit up with joy as I sang that dear song," she told Herb.

Herb went on to state, "When I think of that situation today, I know that Mike no longer has AIDS. He will have a brand new body and he's with the Lord Jesus Christ. I realize that we are all sinners saved by His grace. None of us is worthy, but it's only through the blood of Jesus Christ that we can be saved. He bore the price on the cross for our sins. Mike is now rejoicing in heaven. What an incredible thought!"

AIDS hospices in Southern California have become a second home for Herb Hall. "I go in to see people suffering with HIV and AIDS, and I tell the patients, 'I'm a licensed minister and I have AIDS myself.' That latter comment inevitably gets their attention."

"I don't ask how they got AIDS nor do I share the Gospel with them initially," Herb explained. "First, I want to become their friend. After I've been back two or three times, most of the time people will ask me, 'How is it you're coming here to see me?' Then I tell them, 'Not only do I live with the same disease you do and know what you're going through, but I'm also a Christian.' I'm able to share the Gospel with many people."

THE PANDA BEAR AND THE BIBLE

At one facility in Garden Grove, Herb regularly visited a bedridden AIDS patient. "His name was Don and he was really sick," said Herb, "I remember asking him one day, 'Don, do you know Jesus Christ?' Don turned to me and said brightly, 'Oh yes, I asked the Lord into my heart a couple of days ago.'" He explained that someone had come to see him from the Vineyard Christian Fellowship in Anaheim and had talked with him about the Lord. As a result Don asked the Lord into his life.

"When I went into the room one day, there was another patient there. He was able to move around but he was very fragile looking. I asked him his name and he told me it was Michael. I glanced over to the nightstand and saw a Bible on it. Above his bed, I saw a small wooden cross."

Herb asked, "Michael, do you know Jesus Christ?"

Michael nodded his head. "I used to be a transsexual, but Jesus changed my life," he said. "I can't wait until I can get out of here so I can get back to my church."

"What church is that?" Herb asked him.

"It's the Vineyard," he said.

Herb prayed with him that day, and as he got ready to leave, he turned and said, "Michael, is there anything you would like me to bring you?"

His face lit up again. "Herb, I would like a little panda bear."

And Don added, "I'd like a bag of corn chips."

"Okay," said Herb, "when I come back I'll bring them to you."

"This was on a Tuesday and on Friday, I went shopping and bought a little stuffed panda bear for Michael and a bag of corn chips for Don. I took them to my friends that day. Don said, 'I needed the bigger corn chips. I have trouble eating these little ones.'"

Herb told him that he should keep them as a "back-up" and, when he returned, he would bring "the big ones."

Herb took the panda bear over to Mike, and presented it to him. Tears welled up in his eyes, so Herb said, "Mike, let's come up with a name for him." Without hesitation, he turned and said, "I'm gonna name him, 'O God,' because of what God has done in my life."

Herb had trouble blinking back the tears in his own eyes. "I left that day really touched by the Lord, thinking of the Scripture in Matthew 25 where the Lord, said, '[What] you've done unto the least of these My brethren, you've done unto Me.'"

The following Monday, Herb got a telephone call from a nurse at the facility who told him, "Herb, I have to tell you that the day after you gave Mike the panda bear, he passed away."

Herb's heart sank. "If it had been the other guy in the room, I could have understood because he was the one that looked the sickest," said Herb. "Michael had still been able to get around and was doing things. I was devastated."

The nurse explained, "I didn't want you to walk into the room and see Mike's empty bed and have it hit you like a ton of bricks, so I thought I had better call you."

Herb did return to the room where the two men lived. "I walked in and the panda bear was still on Mike's bed," he recalled. "I looked at the nightstand and Mike's Bible was still there and the little wooden cross was above the bed. That told me that Mike didn't have any family because when a relative dies, people normally come and take all the personal effects out of the room. I reached up and I took down the little wooden cross. I went to the nurse's station and said, 'Mike didn't have any family, did he?' The nurse went on to tell me that he had a distant relative in Oklahoma, but when they called her, she said, 'Just take his garbage and throw it away.' That's what she called it—garbage."

Herb turned to the nurse and said, "Could I have this little wooden cross? It means a lot to me." She nodded her head and began to cry.

" As I stood there, I said to myself, 'You know, God, Mike didn't deserve to die alone.' The Lord spoke to my heart, 'Herb, Mike didn't die alone. I was with Mike when he died and Mike is with Me now.'"

Herb continued to see patients at this facility. One was named Mark. Herb shared with him that he, too, had AIDS.

"We talked for an hour, and when I left I said, 'Mark, is there something you would like for me to bring you?'

"He nodded, 'I would really like to have a Bible.'

"I'd never had an AIDS patient ask for a Bible before and I didn't have the money to buy one.

"I knew that KBRT had been giving away Rainbow Study Bibles as promotionals on the air," said Herb. "I called my friend Tim Berends and said, 'Would KBRT be willing to donate a Bible to this guy with AIDS?'"

"Sure," said the broadcaster. "Come down and get it." Herb asked Tim if he would have all the employees there at the station sign it and write a little note to Mark. Tim thought that was "an excellent idea".

"I went that evening," said Herb, "and picked up the Bible. The staff had filled the front and back of the Bible with little notes and Scripture verses for Mark. I took the Bible to him, and he opened it and started reading the inscriptions. Tears began streaming down his face as he exclaimed, 'These people don't even know me and they love me.'

"I said to myself, 'This is the love of Christ in action.'

"However, Mark's joy was shortlived. I went back to see him a week later and he was close to tears."

"Herb, my Bible's missing," he said, adding, "Who would take my Bible?"

Herb searched through the drawers in the room, but there was no sign of the Bible. "I'm going to call the director," said Mark.

Afterwards, Herb began arrangements to get Mark a new Bible and have people re-sign it. However, when Herb returned two days later, he saw that the original Bible had been found, so a replacement wasn't necessary.

OPEN DOORS

Herb said, "I am thankful for the way God has changed my life. I'm thankful for the doors that I see Him continually opening. Most of all, however, I am thankful to see people who had previously given up hope, give their lives to Jesus Christ. I see their lives change."

Herb emphasizes that we are not all called to an AIDS ministry, but as Christians, we're all called to share the Gospel and reach out to the least, the last, and the lost when we have the opportunity to do so.

"I see my own future in a positive light because I know that, even living with AIDS, I'm having the best days of my life," he said. "I know that if I were to die this very second, I would be in the presence of God. Even living with AIDS today, I know I have eternal life because I'm going to be with Jesus tomorrow."

LOOKING AHEAD

One day, Herb and Bruce were discussing Herb's medical condition. "You know, Bruce," said Herb, "I've only got 53 T-cells left. When I get down to the last one or so, I've decided to give each one of them a name.

"And what are you going to call the last one?" asked Bruce.

"Judas!" said Herb with a grin.

Tamara Brown

Chapter Five

PAINT IT BLACK

Surf City USA—Huntington Beach, California—definitely was not a healthy environment for a teenager in the seventies. As scores of surfers searched for the perfect wave in the Pacific Ocean by the old pier, this beach community in Orange County had also become an arena for drug and alcohol abuse and "free sex" for many of the thousands of young people who lived there. This part of the Golden State definitely tarnished many young lives and Tamara Lindley was no exception.

Tamara, like many of the other kids searching for meaning in their lives, found that this surfers' paradise turned into a living hell because of the temptations it provided. At an early age, she began to "paint it black." Not to have participated, she felt, would have marked her as "different" and she didn't want to be that. So this "wild hawk" with a bubbly, effervescent personality became a rebel without a cause, and that rebellion has since come back to haunt her. Now she is married, in her thirties, and she has a young son. Tamara was born in Santa Monica, California, and raised in Westchester, California, until the age of four-and-a-half, when the family moved to Huntington Beach.

"I started kindergarten at a school one block from my house and finished high school at Huntington Beach High School," she said. "I was a typical teenager in that I was a bit of a rebel."

"My parents were basically upper middle class, owned their own business, went to work every day and left me in the care of my grandmother who lived with us. Grandma was my caregiver and raised me. Eventually I lost her to a convalescent home because she was very old when I was born, and eventually she could no longer take care of herself or me."

Tamara was left with nobody to look after her. "I also have a brother three-and-a-half years older than me who still lives in Southern California. He is more of a studious individual, where I was more the outgoing, social type of person," she said.

Nothing was ever "enough" for Tamara, a vivacious young lady that attracted the attention of the boys at school and on the beach. With no one to check her, she always wanted more out of life.

"I was always seeking something else to do, to occupy me and stimulate my interest and feelings," she admitted. "I was continually attempting to reach for the stars in everything I did. I was not comfortable with myself and I was searching for affirmation from others. I guess that's what caused me to start drinking and using 'recreational' drugs at such an early age."

Tamara says she had her first taste of marijuana when she was only nine years of age. "It wasn't a constant thing, but it became more regular as the years went by," she declared. She said that while living in Huntington Beach which was "the drug capital of Southern California", she was offered her "first smoke" by her older friends.

"We thought drugs was where the excitement was," she recalled. "It was something that was forbidden and exciting, and even at nine, I already was seeking that out. My first rendezvous with drugs took place after school on the playground," she recalled.

Because of her "free spirit," Tamara began being attracted to boys at school during the first grade. "Everything was early with me," she declared. "By the age of thirteen, I was doing drugs every day. I was either drinking, smoking pot, taking some sort of pill, or experimenting with LSD. By my freshman year, it was non-stop. I took something to give me a 'high' every day."

"This eventually curtailed my enjoyment of going to school," she continued. "I started having truancy problems. My parents were called in by the school, but by then I was out of control. They could do little or nothing to bring me into line."

"By my sophomore year, I started running away from home. I would be gone for two weeks at a time which was driving my parents absolutely batty, but I didn't care because I was in a race— running with no direction."

Tamara described her mother and father as being "the yuppies of the seventies," adding, "There was no mother at home, they owned a business and my parents were caught up in that."

She went on: "They wanted this business together and I guess I was a little jealous of that."

So with her parents running an all-consuming company and attending conventions across America, Tamara said she was left to her own devices. That turned out to be extremely dangerous at that formative period of her life.

"By the age of fifteen-and-a-half, I was already engaged in sex," she said. "I had some medical problems where I didn't have a typical menstrual cycle, so I was protected against pregnancy which gave me the go-ahead. I was looking for acceptance, too, as I searched for that boyfriend, that special relationship. I thought that sleeping with guys would give me that."

On reflection, Tamara believes she was actually trying to replace the void that only Jesus Christ could fill in her life. "I was really trying to fill the emptiness, the loneliness—trying to find excitement and constantly looking for new things to do," she said.

Surprisingly, in view of her behavior, Tamara attended Sunday School when she was a young girl. "What happened was that my parents didn't continue going to church," she explained, "They started dropping me and my brother off on Sundays and then they went home to rest because of their weariness from working so hard at their business, so I knew a little bit about Jesus. I attended the local church camps in summer up to about the age of fourteen, but there was a lot of partying at the church camps, too.

"I went to camp in the San Bernardino mountains as a volunteer dishwasher and food preparer when I was about fourteen years old, and we were all partying. I received several mixed messages there. I really think my parents were blinded (at least to a certain degree) to what I was doing in the early days."

To pay for her own habit, Tamara began dealing drugs. "I was pushing more and more to get something out of my life," she said. "I wanted 'the James Dean' type of rebel boyfriend—anything that would make me think, *This is something new and neat.*"

Despite her many difficulties, Tamara was able to graduate from Huntington Beach High School in 1978 with a 3.0 average.

THE GERMS

In the late seventies and early eighties, Los Angeles became a mega-center for rock and roll music and quite naturally, Tamara was attracted to the glamor of it. "There was excitement and a false type of dreamworld in being involved with the different bands," she recalled. "There were many late nights for me."

The bands she followed had names like The Germs, Black Flag, Fear, The Bags, The Alice Bag Band, The Castration Squad, and an all-woman group—Sex Sick. The weirdest band she associated with was Christian Death, something Tamara knew all about in her own life.

Was she, I wondered, a groupie who attended the concerts and then slept with the band members?

"No, I never was," she said. "I was too old to be a groupie. I never cared about having sex with the band members. I just wanted to party, and many times, I brought my own drugs. I had a way of being able to attain friendship by being more than a groupie. I didn't give my 'all' to the lead singer. If we engaged in any type of physical activity, it wasn't like, 'He's mine now,' or 'I'm his girl.' It was something that was done along with drugs and alcohol. If it was fun, you did it." Tamara says that often she left with the member of the band talking about "good old rock 'n' roll" and the great artists of the past.

She went to popular venues like The Troubadour or The Starwood. "I used to go every Tuesday and Wednesday nights while I was still employed, and I would 'do' some speed to get me to work the next morning," she recalled. "I'd be at the Tropicana or one of the other local motels where the artists stayed. I'd stay and party most of the night. After an hour's sleep, I'd get up and go to work." She was definitely burning the candle at both ends. Tamara admits she went wherever she thought the "action" would be.

"One night, I was in Pomona at Toxic Shock, a record store, partying in the back. I had taken some liquid LSD mixed with heroin. We were in a closed room—about ten of us together as a group," she recalled. "Some of these people were from the 'crypt' itself. They had this huge, huge snake there. The thing must have been twenty feet long and it was in a cage above a bed. In a corner was an altar of petrified animals. My flesh began to crawl and I was blown away by all of this. This was pretty strange even for me."

"On top of this they had a dungeon, a torture chamber. One of the guys and his girlfriend were making a 'move' on me. I was kind of flirtatious with it, but that was as far as I wanted to go."

This bizarre experience became a "big stop sign" for Tamara despite the fact that her boyfriend at the time was bisexual. "You know, there was this guy trying to put a 'make' on my boyfriend," she said. "It was getting a little too confusing for me, but I was living an 'anything goes' lifestyle."

I asked Tamara if there were times when she had some close calls with drugs. "I had a few real scares," Tamara admits. "I almost overdosed on morphine pills one night at the Fleetwood, a concert hall in Redondo Beach. In the back of the hall, I began sweating bullets," she said.

Most of the time, however, Tamara says she was able to "handle" her drugs. "People would look at me and never know I was on stuff," Tamara said. "Several times I actually 'fried' on LSD in front of my parents, and they didn't even know what was going on. Amazing." Tamara describes that period in her life as being the "insane years."

Not surprisingly, the police began to figure regularly in Tamara's life. She recalls being in a record store one evening—it was a front for a drug ring—when it got raided. "I was loaded on LSD and heroin when they forced open the front door and dashed in," she remembers. "When this occurred most of the people were high on drugs or drunk. I managed to escape out of the back of the store. The scene at the time was psycho city."

On another occasion, she was at an "anything goes" bar in Redondo Beach. "I was only nineteen years old, so I was a minor," she said. I had carried fake ID since I was sixteen. "I knew I was in trouble when the police arrived. In fact, a bunch of us in the bar were minors, and we were 'doing the down and out' on Quaaludes and a lot of alcohol.

"Anyway, the bar was raided and we began to run through this little passageway into the back trying to escape the police, but they had surrounded the place and weren't allowing anybody out. The bar staff told us to try and hide with our backs flat against the back wall of the building."

"HALT, OR WE'LL SHOOT!"

Some of the minors made a headlong plunge out the back door and headed for the nearest fence, ready to scramble over it at the rear of the lot. As Tamara attempted to scale the fence with a girlfriend, she heard a voice shout, "Halt, or I'll shoot!"

Not thinking clearly, the two of them took their chances and got over the fence. "There was a door open in an apartment complex nearby, so we ran up the stairs to the second story and into the apartment where a group of people were partying," she recalled. "We actually barged into the early seventies. Inside, was a group of long-haired rock and rollers, so we stayed with them, partying with people we'd never met before. This was the lifestyle and antics that were the norm for me," said Tamara.

The group that Tamara associated with shared information with each other about the location of parties and places to "crash." A friend would say, "Tamara, we've found a great place to sleep." Up to twelve people, all high on drugs, would sleep on the floor of a place they had just walked into uninvited.

"Quite often we didn't know the name of the owner of the apartment or even what town we were in," she said. "I could have been a 'night stalker' and they would never have known."

THE FLOPHOUSE

Tamara recalls staying at a "flophouse" in Redondo Beach which had been a youth center and had been converted into spartan quarters with small, individual rooms stuffed with mattresses reeking of mildew.

"I spent a lot of time there from about age nineteen through my early twenties," Tamara recalled. "We were punks with our strange hairstyles and clothes and manner of living. We would listen to music all night, share everything we had and steal what we didn't have, not from individuals but from the local convenience stores."

Tamara also spent time around the gay community. "The gays had a lot of good drugs and they were fun to be around," she said. You didn't have to worry about the 'make' or anything, so when I chose to stay celibate (I did go through a little bit of time of wanting to be just that), I would hang around with them."

Tamara recalled the evening when she was with some friends in Long Beach, home of the Queen Mary and a wide variety of bars. In one of them, Tamara took a tremendous amount of speed and then drank a fifth of tequila along with a case of beer. "It was the time of the Long Beach Grand Prix and I began giggling helplessly and running around the area like a maniac, stealing flags from the race site," she recalled.

"We broke into a park that was closed and climbed up the trees and jumped off branches and onto the ground and we ran around like crazy people."

Tamara remembers   suddenly being surrounded by police patrol cars with guns pointed at the group. Her car was there and being driven on the lawn of the park by somebody else.

"I was so stoned that I didn't even know my name that night," she said. "We all took off running when the police came. They eventually caught us. I can't remember what was said or anything else but amazingly, they didn't arrest any of us. It always seemed like I was skating on thin ice—but surviving, getting away with things."

There were other occasions when Tamara couldn't believe that she got away with her brushes with the law. "One insane evening, we were driving all over Long Beach, dropping off people, and stopping for another drink or whatever drug was available," she said. "I had started home, and all of a sudden the car lurched to a stop outside my house. I had driven twenty miles and yet I was so zoned out that I couldn't park my car. It was stuck diagonally against the curb. I started reversing out into the street. All of a sudden, I was blearily aware of a flashing red light behind me."

Worse for wear, Tamara hissed to herself, "I don't believe this. This is not happening. I drove all this way, but I can't park my car."

After what seemed like an eternity, there came the inevitable tap on the window, and a burly police office said, "Hi."

With this, Tamara began to bawl hysterically. "I live here, I really do," she sobbed through her frustration. "I can't get my car to go straight. All I want to do is go inside."

Tamara said that her hysteria was play acting. "I guess it was a little bit of a con. I knew exactly what I was doing," she recalled.

The officer stared at her in disgust and was not deterred, however. "May I see your license?" he asked firmly. He didn't trust anybody, even the hysterical woman before him.

Tamara desperately searched through her bag for it, but it couldn't be found. "It was incredible," she said. "Instead of being arrested—he could have gotten me for substance abuse, big time, I had drank so much and done so many drugs—he parked my car for me, helped me to my door and I went inside."

Tamara wasn't always that fortunate and there were times she did get arrested. "I always seemed to get caught on the most mellow nights of my life," she said. "Like the time I'd polished off a case of beer in Laguna Beach. Then in the car on the way back with a friend named Donny, I drank a bottle of ready-mix Manhattan.

"It was just before Christmas in 1981 and it was very foggy." So, in her befuddled state and with the mist swirling around in huge tentacles making it difficult to see the road ahead, she began to see everything in triple.

Tamara asked her companion to drive and she pulled over to the side of the road and flashed on the emergency lights so they could make the switch. When she glanced over at Donny, she said, "Oops, I guess not." Donny was "toast"—he was gone. So she decided to sit there for a while trying to gather her thoughts as her head woozily rolled on her fragile shoulders.

"Well, guess who comes behind me and raps on the door. A police officer," she said. "I had been really stupid that night. I had forgotten to pull the keys out of the ignition. I knew I was too drunk to drive home, yet the officer pulled me out, and I passed most of the sobriety tests. But then, my high heels let me down as I tried to walk. I slipped and fell back into the policeman's arms."

Tamara, not surprisingly, spent the night in the "slammer" and appeared in court the next day where she plead guilty to a drunk driving charge.

On another occasion, Tamara was arrested and held in a cell after doing base cocaine in Pasadena. "On the way home, the car I was traveling in was pulled over because my friend had faulty plates on her car," she said. "The police checked and discovered that I had forgotten to pay a speeding ticket and they arrested me on a warrant."

"I could have been arrested for dealing drugs or for purse snatching when I was on the street. Or even for 'dining and dashing' which I did quite regularly to survive. I would order a meal, eat it and then run out without paying. If I'd had money, I would have willingly paid for it, plus giving a good hefty tip."

Fortunately for her, Tamara only spent short periods in jail. "I would be in jail for a week here and there," she recalled. "I was once picked up at a party when I was very young and put in the Orange County Jail, and then I was released. I don't know if I would have 'lasted' long in prison, but then, maybe I would have liked it because I would have had a home, a permanent home.

"Believe it or not, a lot of people like jail. That's why they repeat to get back inside. They get healthcare and three meals a day. Strangely enough, they also get lots of love in prison. There are the physical acts, but also I think there's a camaraderie between those in prison. When I was in jail, even for a few days, we'd start sharing stories and having lots of fun."

A SUGAR DADDY

I wondered how Tamara managed to pay for all the drugs she was consuming. "Women don't have to pay for drugs," she asserted. "They do other things. I've heard some women say, 'Well, I never was a prostitute.' But those of us out on the street do prostitute ourselves in one way or another to survive. When I was on the run and needed a place to live, I had one man who was basically a caretaker of mine, a sugar daddy, and I gave him sex for financial stability."

"I was never, however, a street prostitute. That's one thing I never had to do. I believed that I'm basically an intelligent person and I would reason, 'Why should I become a street prostitute for thirty bucks when I can have a sugar daddy for five hundred?' I made sure that I was his and his alone. He had me and he had his girlfriend. I was his toy.

"I figured that a lot of women sleep with somebody for dinner, then go home. You'd have wine and a nice dinner, and then you would go to bed, and you wake up and go home. He might or might not call you the next time. I knew that I would get five hundred dollars at least each occasion I spent some time with this man. I had no emotional attachment to him. A few days later, he would call again and I'd make some more money."

In this way, Tamara could support whatever drug she happened to choose at the time. Still, she wondered how long she could continue this insane lifestyle.

Her answer was not long in coming.

Chapter Six

SICK AND TIRED
OF BEING SICK AND TIRED

Each day, Tamara's heart fluttered as she approached a nearby liquor store with its stock of elixir that could provide her with a temporary escape. She believed it was indispensable to help her forget her emptiness.

The lure that the adult bookstore held for Herb Hall, was similar to hers, but for a different reason. The draw of the liquor store was irresistible for Tamara in her topsy-turvy world. Once she had secured the liquor bottle that she carried in her oversized purse, it then became a race with time to empty its contents down her throat. Her hands shook tremulously as she greedily gulped down the palliative liquid.

She had become fixated on anything that helped her dull her senses. Like many alcoholics, she became expert in disguising her intoxicated state from those around her.

"I could consume a twelve-pack of beer and was still able to function," she stated. "I was an alcoholic, but what was beginning to occur was that when I got sober each morning, I began to feel sick and tired of being sick and tired."

Tamara also was getting weary of waking up after sleeping with some man she wouldn't even have had a meal with if she had been sober. Her lifestyle was causing her to scrutinize her tortured soul.

"I was so demoralized by the music scene and what went along with it that it really helped me to give up all my drug and alcohol props," she recalled, a hint of sadness in her voice.

"My last choice of drugs was alcohol," she recalled. "I had quit doing a lot of hallucinogens by my early twenties. I had even cut down on cocaine. However, I did get involved with a lot of crystal toward the end, because it was cheaper. You could get higher on it and the effects lasted much longer which meant I could drink more."

However, the drugs were taking a toll on her life. "I'd be doing eight balls of crystal speed with my friend when I was used to doing eight balls of cocaine. Still, I found it didn't have the intensity it use to," she said. "The problem was that nothing was ever enough for me. I always felt there had to be something else," she added.

During her rare moments of sober reflection, Tamara grasped the last shred of her mind as she began to ruminate over her future. It looked pretty grim. "I looked inside myself and all I saw was black," she said.

Her accommodations in this period of her life ranged from living out of her car one night to staying in someone's San Marino mansion or on the King's Road in Hollywood the next. Then she would return to sleeping on someone's couch or in her car.

"It was an up-and-down lifestyle," she recalled. "I found that when I was down, I was really down, but when I was up, man, I was on top of the world. One moment, I'd be almost broke, counting my pennies for tomato soup or something out of a can that I could eat, then I'd be eating a seven-course dinner at one of the finest restaurants on La Cienega in L.A. with a distinguished gentleman."

This erratic lifestyle was really burning Tamara out. "It began to catch up with me," she said. "I saw other people having a normal life and I wondered what made them that way."

Tamara repeated that she eventually got tired of being sick and tired. "I was tired of being abused," she said, "sick of sleeping with everybody I met. Every time I met a new guy who showed interest in me, I would think, *This is it.* Then, within a month, the relationship would be over. Sometimes, he just disappeared out of my life."

"TAMARA, YOU'RE NOT AN ALCOHOLIC"

One of Tamara's boyfriends at this time was a "recovering alcoholic" who attended a local Alcoholics Anonymous twelve-step program. "The problem was that he wanted me to stay sick so he told me, 'Tamara, you're not an alcoholic,' but all the evidence pointed to the fact that I was. I mean, for goodness' sake," she said, "I poured every type of booze into my body, but still, he kept saying that."

Tamara's liquid diet included anything from a case of beer and a fifth of whiskey, to just a six-pack in an evening. "It was whatever was around," she remembers. "If I had a six-pack that would have to do because it was all I could afford. I was always in a state of some sort of euphoria or drunkenness."

Tamara somehow managed to stay employed—it was the one feather in her cap. "I would never drink at work," she said. "I quit drinking at seven in the morning when I arrived on the job. Maybe I had gotten an hour's sleep—sometimes no sleep at all, and then I'd wait for four o'clock or five o'clock in the afternoon when I'd get off work. I immediately went out and bought some booze and picked up a 'cork' immediately."

"I desperately wanted to believe my boyfriend's prognosis because I didn't really want to come to terms with my addiction. I moved in with him, and enviously watched him in his sobriety and as he attended the local A.A. meetings."

Meanwhile, there was another roommate in the house where she was staying. "I always lived in a communal setting," Tamara explained. "There were always half a dozen people in the house where I was staying. I was talking to this woman one day and I started telling her about my past, and she responding by saying, 'Tamara, read this book. I guess I'm not supposed to say it, but I think you're an alcoholic—a chronic alcoholic.'"

Tamara protested her statement. "My boyfriend says that I'm not an alcoholic."

The woman allowed a knowing smile to cross her face. "Of course he would say that," she told Tamara. "He wants you to stay sick so he can have control over you."

Confused with the mixed messages she was receiving, Tamara began reading the book, which was the "big book" of Alcoholics Anonymous. It was then that she realized that she was, indeed, an alcoholic. Her three-month relationship with her male friend ended when he went out and drank again and stopped going to the A.A. meetings. "Incidentally, I did go without alcohol for almost two-and-a-half months then, but I was still popping pills," she remembers. "I found that I needed to stay in some sort of 'out-of-me' state. The problem was I never wanted to look at myself in the cold light of day."

"What happened was that, after two and a half months of no alcohol (the day before my boyfriend and I decided to end our relationship), I went out with some old friends and drank like there was no tomorrow."

"I got scared with what drink was doing to me and vowed that I didn't want to do this any more. I was tired of looking inside myself and seeing nothing but black."

Shortly, after they broke up, Tamara went to her first meeting of Alcoholics Anonymous, and has never taken a drink or drugs since then.

Tamara said that first night of abstinence was extremely difficult. "I was sitting on my hands and sweating bullets," she recalled.

"I'M TAMARA—A RECOVERING ALCOHOLIC"

Tamara began attending A.A. meetings regularly, sometimes three times a day at different Orange County locations. "They were all over the county," she stated. "The first meeting I went to —June 22, 1985—was in Garden Grove. It was a 'Newcomers Meeting,' and I got up and said that my name was Tamara and that I was an 'alcoholic'."

"They gave me a wonderful welcome. It was the first time in my life that I had felt welcome no matter who I was or what I had done. All I had to do was show up and I knew I would be loved."

At these meetings, Tamara met people who didn't care about her past sins. "They didn't care whether I was rich or poor," she stated. "These people didn't care what religion I believed in."

At the A.A. meetings, Tamara learned how to live soberly. "They gave me a good foundation of living life one day at a time," she said. "I discovered how to turn my life over to 'the God of my understanding.' Still, I had a problem with that because I had this 'Jesus factor' in my subconscious from my childhood. He was the one I knew as God."

Tamara continued attending the A.A. meetings, and she met a man who was also a regular attendee. "He was much younger than I was yet we stayed together for two years," she said.

Tamara admits that, in her "sick mind," she still engaged in her debauchery-type behavior. "It was sex, unlimited sex, unlimited flirtation, anything that would 'fix me'," she said. "Maybe I didn't drink or do drugs, but I did other things to fill me up."

Tamara ultimately realized that the point of the A.A. program was God. "The problem was I hadn't looked for the God of absolutes—the God of the Bible."

Still, she began reading her Bible. "I was engaging in extra-marital sex and everything, and the guilt that was consuming me was incredible," she said. "Afterwards, I would feel ill."

The turning point came for Tamara when she attended a week-long seminar in Long Beach given by a Christian teacher. "It was called a Basic Youth Seminar," she recalled. "It was really good, but I couldn't make it through the week because what was being taught was convicting me too much. I went for three days and the speaker started talking about the sex thing. I had to leave. He was talking about the family unit and the way that God intended us to be. I had never heard this before."

Tamara's own involvement in sex was too much for her to face. "I didn't want to listen to what was being said, so I didn't return," she said. "However, I started to say to my boyfriend, 'I want to go to church,' but he was against that, feeling I needed to stay longer in the program of A.A."

"He was trying to control me," she recalled.

Tamara had been his girlfriend for quite awhile, but she told him that she couldn't agree with his anti-church feelings.

"Well, if you won't start going to church, I can't see you anymore," Tamara told him one evening. "I really feel I need to go back to church."

She made it clear that she was willing to give him up if his conclusion was so important to him. "I'll miss you but, as for me I need to go to church," she asserted. "I'm willing to give you up and allow you time in whatever you need, but I need to follow what my heart is telling me."

For Tamara, it was the turning point of her life.

Chapter Seven

THE POWER OF PRAYER

Tamara thought she had experienced everything there was in life, but God had a surprise in mind for her. What was about to take place topped anything she had ever experienced in her short, but colorful, life. Maybe it took something dramatic to transform her from an insecure woman into a dynamic disciple of Jesus Christ.

Many who come to a full Christian commitment make that life-changing decision by "going forward" at a Billy Graham crusade. Possibly, they make a decision at a Greg Laurie Monday-night Bible study at nearby Calvary Chapel of Costa Mesa, where the Southern California part of the "Jesus Movement" was birthed in the late sixties and early seventies. But, for Tamara, the sensational supernatural experience occurred not in front of a large audience in Costa Mesa but in the privacy of her own apartment just a stone's throw from Calvary Chapel. It was so dramatic that it would change her life forever.

She described it in this way: "I was home alone one night reading the Bible on my bed and praying, when God suddenly and with a powerful force, came at me with such supernatural power that I was knocked off the bed and fell to the floor. I don't know how long I lay there, but when I woke up, I was praying, and I didn't know what had happened to me."

"However, as I look back, I realize that it was what I needed to clear my soul. I didn't really know how to pray," she went on. "Before this, I had done it tongue-in-cheek. My prayers sounded real good because I knew they were pleasing to people's ears. I've always had an eloquent speaking ability. I had learned to please people as a con artist on the street, but you can't con God, so He showed me His power. I've never been the same since."

When she came around, lying there on the floor of her apartment, Tamara was totally amazed with what had just happened to her. "Four hours had gone by, and it felt like two minutes," she recalled. "I felt totally invigorated and I felt I had all the energy in the world."

BORN AGAIN

"It was incredible," she said. "I now believe John 3:7 in which Jesus said, 'Ye must be born again.'" Tamara said she felt like she had gone through a "birthing process."

After being "born-again," Tamara began attending church again. "I went to a local church and started attending Bible study on Sundays and going regularly on weeknights," she said.

Her boyfriend happened to call her shortly after this experience and she told him what had happened to her. He agreed to accompany her to church and soon, he too, found the Lord and gave his life to Jesus Christ.

"Today this friend has graduated from Bible School and is planning to be a minister," she recounted. "Our relationship lasted another year and a half. Sadly, we fought a lot. He was much younger than me. I wanted different things, like getting married and having a child. I wanted to start our family unit. I believed God wanted this for my life. He wasn't ready, but he would never let me break up with him. I guess we were just comfortable with each other."

"While I was still seeing this man, I went to a singles' retreat because I felt I needed a vacation," she said. "I hadn't vacationed in years. I now had a job at an insurance company after being a receptionist at a hair salon for some time. I had a steady job. A great job. Benefits. Everything! I was finally in the realm of the mainstream. It was great! I also didn't have the fear of drinking or taking drugs any more. Sex had also been removed from my life. The Lord was everything to me. I was totally overwhelmed."

A LITTLE ORNAMENT

After navigating the steep highway up to the San Bernardino mountains with its hairpin bends, Tamara arrived safely at the mountain-top retreat. She opened the trunk of her car and began carrying her suitcases to the reception area. As she did, she breathed in the pure air, bringing with it the refreshing scent of pine trees.

"All of a sudden this swarthy six-foot man with dark hair appeared and said, 'Let me take them for you,' It was Gary Brown. I looked at him with mute surprise. No one had ever done that for me before," Tamara went on, "not even the person I was seeing. I seemed to be an ornament for him which he'd take down when he wanted to see it and dust it off. I accepted that because that's how I was always treated by the men in my life."

A girlfriend who was with Tamara at the time introduced the two of them. "It felt good, but weird," she recalled. "Gary carried the bags to my room."

A few days later, Tamara was in the retreat bookstore when they met again. "Jesus was something new to me and I needed reading material to find out more about Him. I felt I needed more than the Bible because sometimes you need all the flavors," she said. "Gary started pointing out different commentaries which he recommended for me to read. He suggested books by J. Vernon McGee which he felt were easy to read, and he picked up one of them and said, 'This would be a good one to start with.'"

Gary went on to suggest some other books which he said would give Tamara "much more depth"—books penned by Andrew Murray.

"Gary took the time to explain to me sweetly and gently without judging me for not knowing or being ignorant of certain facts about the Christian walk," recalled Tamara. "He made me feel that I didn't have to worry about having to measure up to some impossible standard."

As he towered above her, Tamara found herself praying, "Lord, if this is the man You have selected for me, I'd be real happy for life."

The pair spent some quality time together and became good friends. "Nothing more. Nothing less," she recalled. "It apparently couldn't go any further because I was already seeing somebody else, and even though I could wish or dream of being involved with Gary, this relationship could not lead to anything else, I felt," she said.

On the last day at the idyllic retreat, Tamara told Gary, "It has meant so much to me to have met you up here, and I cherish you so much as a friend." Gary was touched with her words and then they hugged and said goodbye.

Tamara revealed that she called Gary periodically. "Not every day, but every other week, and I'd tell him about some of the problems I was having with the man I was seeing," she said. "Gary would listen and then say, 'Tamara, you need to seek the Lord and pray about this. But I must say that God doesn't want you to be abused. God needs you to be edified and drawn closer to Him instead of having this constant turmoil in your life.'"

Tamara said that during the time he spent on the phone with her, Gary never once said, "Oh honey, get over here right now." She appreciated that because she was very vulnerable at the time.

"He never once took advantage of me, or showed the crude manners of my previous boyfriends," she said.

Three months after the retreat, Tamara felt it was time for her to break up with her boyfriend. "I left that weekend," she said. "I didn't date or see him. I called him on the Sunday evening and told him, 'I'm sorry, but our relationship is not working out.' I knew that I had to break up with him over the phone because he would never let me end the relationship in person. It was hard for me because this was the most permanent relationship I had ever had."

The couple had been going steady for two years—this was a lifetime for Tamara. "It had been the most intense, consistent relationship I'd had with a man and I was a little scared about the breakup because I knew I would no longer have a Saturday-night date." She felt a wave of anxiety wash over her.

Tamara's father, when he heard that she had ended the relationship, told his daughter, "Tamara, go out and date some people with some substance." So she decided to try and heed his advice.

"I began dating a lot of people," she stated. "I went out with various men for lunch. There was no sex, just dating. Still, I didn't feel good about it."

On top of this uneasiness, Tamara said she had a problem going to the local church because that was where her ex-boyfriend attended.

"I showed up once and couldn't sit still. I had to leave," she admitted. "I started attending a different church, but that didn't feel right, either."

In the meantime, Tamara felt the need to be baptized. So, one sunny day, she joined hundreds of other new converts at Pirates Cove by Corona del Mar Beach. These mass baptisms came to be a regular summer event and were organized by Calvary Chapel of

Costa Mesa. Many people lined the rocks (including Gary) to watch these new believers wade into the ocean. Upon their confession of faith in Jesus Christ, they were "dunked" in this age-old tradition.

Shortly after this wonderful event, and with the problem of her ex-boyfriend weighing heavily on her heart, she called Gary. "Gary, can you meet me at the singles' fellowship tonight, please?" she asked. He agreed and, with a group of other singles, they shared a Coke in a local restaurant. Afterwards, they sat in Gary's car, and talked incessantly.

"I just felt really good; I was very attracted to him, but I still considered him a friend," she remembers. "He asked me out to a Christian rock concert the next night and, as I accepted, I felt like a schoolgirl going out on her first date."

Having been hurt so many times before, Tamara confessed that she felt the need to keep a firm wedge between the two of them. "I guess I wasn't yet ready for a new relationship," she explained. "I had just broken up a month before with my boyfriend. I was platonically dating other men at the same time, too."

One of Gary's friends also told him to "cruise it" with Tamara. "Slow down and don't get too involved with her," he advised.

Still, they were both aware that something special was happening in their lives. "It was magical, and what was strange is that when I was up at the retreat center, God had 'told' me that somehow I would end up marrying this wonderful man."

Gary and Tamara continued to see each other every day. "No one had ever cared for me like he did," she said.

To further complicate the relationship, Tamara came down with a chronic illness. "It wouldn't go away," she recalled. "I didn't seem to be able to fight this infection."

As Tamara lay shivering in her bed one night, Gary calmly opened the door to her room and closed it gently behind him. "He looked at the two blankets on my bed and was shocked," she said. "I had cold chills from the fever and had no comforter to help me to keep warm."

He commented, "No wonder you're sick." He went straight to a local store and bought me a comforter and matching pillows."

To further show his concern, he also rang her front doorbell and dropped roses off on her doorstep. "I'd never had this treatment before and I didn't think I deserved it," Tamara said. "In fact, I tried to test it a little bit with arguments, but it never worked. He wouldn't go away."

By December, three months after they had started dating, Gary and Tamara made a trip to the mountains again. "We'd gone up to a Christmas singles' retreat," she said, "and we took a small excursion to Big Bear City. He bought me a little ruby ring and said, 'I know you've been left by a lot of different men, but this is a "promise" ring telling you that one day we'll be engaged to be married. I'm not going away, Tamara.' Because he knew my past where there had never been permanency in my relationships, he gave me that ring as we were standing by the lake. Gary picked the most beautiful place for professing his love."

Tamara thought that they would be engaged by the following August, but she said, "The Lord had different things in mind."

On January 18, 1988, Gary called Tamara at her job at the insurance company where she was the switchboard operator. "He told me before that he had been looking at rings, but he didn't have the money to pay for any of them," she stated. "But this day, when he called, he said, 'Tamara, I've got the money.'"

In other words, he was asking her to become his wife. "What a place to do it," she laughed. "I was on the switchboard so I couldn't scream. In fact, I couldn't do anything. I just sat there and all the color drained out of my face. I fell out of my chair with the headset still on."

The following Saturday night, they purchased the engagement ring and went to celebrate at the Spaghetti Bender, a restaurant in Newport Beach. "It was moderately priced which was good for both our incomes," said Tamara.

Gary talked about his version of his life story. He said he was born in Arcadia, California, and when he was eight, he moved to Walnut where he lived for eight years. After attending Roland Heights High School for two years, his family moved to Lido Island in swanky Newport Beach, California, one of the wealthiest areas of Orange County.

"I ended up being with rich people and I really got in with the wrong crowd," he said. "I started taking drugs when we moved there . I graduated from Newport Harbor High School in 1975."

"My dad owned his own company from the bottom up, and I was a rich boy living in a rich family, doing a lot of pot and also a lot of drinking in high school."

Gary found himself on the wrong end of the law with drunk driving violations, but he had a rich father, who always bailed him out.

"He hired the best lawyers to get me out of the charges," Gary recalled. "I had four successive charges and, after the fourth, the judge told me, 'Young man, either you quit drinking or I'll throw you in jail.'"

Gary said he was tired of drinking and "doing drugs." Suddenly, a drinking buddy "accepted the Lord." Gary was astonished at the way his life immediately changed for the better. "He just quit smoking pot and drinking, and gave himself over to the Lord."

His friend took Gary to a succession of Saturday-night concerts at Calvary Chapel of Costa Mesa. "I finally accepted the Lord at a Darrell Mansfield concert," he said. "Then a year later, I went to the Calvary Chapel Bible school at Twin Peaks. It was a great experience—studying the Bible and everything. After the school was over, I worked at Twin Peaks for a whole summer. I was a maintenance person on the grounds. Then I came back here to Orange County and worked in a Bible bookstore. My father bought me a house in Costa Mesa and I attended Calvary Chapel three or four times a week. I also went to the church retreats all the time. They were weekend retreats and week-long retreats."

Gary recalls meeting Tamara for the first time at Twin Peaks. "We were just friends, and when we came back from the mountains, we just fellowshipped together and I got to know her," he said.

I wondered why Gary was so attracted to Tamara. "It was her free spirit and her transparent honesty," he said as pride shone in his eyes. "Tamara wanted to do everything with the Lord. She was such a beautiful person. The Lord shone through her. She put the Lord first."

Now, soon, they would link lives together "for better or for worse."

Chapter Eight

"FOR BETTER, FOR WORSE"

The clock was ticking and it was fast approaching midday on Saturday, October 15, 1988, when Tamara Lindley was to become Tamara Lindley Brown. Tamara had long dreamed of the day when she would marry her sweet and kind Gary. About a hundred family and friends began entering the large haven of Calvary Chapel to witness the great event.

As Tamara was being driven in a rented towncar to the huge facility, she found herself experiencing a strange mixture of emotions. Tamara was happy that she and Gary would at last be able to formally pledge their love for each other "... for better, for worse," but she was also afraid that she would fluff her lines.

Suddenly she was at the church! As the organist began to play "The Wedding March," all eyes turned toward her as she slowly began her march down the aisle in a beautiful white wedding dress, its long train billowing out behind her.

When Tamara arrived at Gary's side, he gasped at how lovely she looked, her long auburn hair framing her face in soft curls. They looked at each other and nearly broke into tears of joy.

The church had been beautifully decorated with flowers for the great occasion and Tamara's green eyes locked on the huge wooden dove that dominated the front wall of the sanctuary. It signified peace—a peace she finally found when she surrendered her life to Jesus Christ.

Vic Shmeltz, one of the church's many pastors, took his place in front of the couple, as they were flanked by Stan, the best man, and Lori, the maid of honor.

"We chose these two people because they were the ones who had the most to do with teaching us about the Lord," explained Tamara. "Stan had known Gary for several years. I had met Lori at my place of employment when I looked kind of like Marilyn Monroe. I was then working on 'cleaning up my act,' and Lori talked to me about Jesus a little bit because she knew I wanted to know Him so much. When I was hungry, she'd invite me over for dinner having shown me true Christian love."

Pastor Vic was also a great ally to the two of them. Gary confided in him one day that he planned to marry Tamara, but they would first be engaged for a year. "That is good," he responded. "Tamara's a very nice girl."

Gary and Tamara had taken marriage classes at Calvary Chapel on Tuesday evenings. "We even paid attention to things we didn't want to hear," she recalled. "We were ready, willing and able to be taught, or at least advised, and we even went for marriage counseling, but Pastor Vic only wanted to see us a few sessions because we'd already gone through an intense class."

Before the wedding, the young pastor had taken an extraordinary interest in Gary and Tamara and even invited them over to his home for "potlucks" and Christmas celebrations.

"So, when the big day finally came, it was like he was marrying close friends, and he had no reservations," she said.

Tamara experienced the ultimate "high" as the pastor went through the wedding vows with each of them and then said, "I now pronounce you man and wife," adding, "Gary, you may now kiss the bride."

"Oohs" and "aahs" broke out from the audience as thirty-two-year-old Gary, wearing a smart gray tuxedo, leaned over and planted a passionate kiss on the Cupid-bow mouth of his beautiful new wife, now twenty-eight years of age. At that heart-stopping moment, Tamara knew beyond a shadow of doubt that nothing would prevent her happiness. Their love had been sealed with a kiss!

The unadorned wedding reception took place at a nearby barn on the grounds of the historic White Newland House in Huntington Beach. "We had sandwiches and salad, and a simple basket-weave-style cake with Precious Moments on top," said Tamara. "From two until about four-thirty, we had a few speeches, and there was some music and a little bit of dancing. There was a real feeling of peace—God's peace—at that wonderful event," she added.

After a honeymoon cruise to the Mexican Riviera, Tamara and Gary returned home to a three-bedroom house in Mesa Verde with a two-car garage, in an exclusive area of Costa Mesa where the value of the land was that of diamonds elsewhere.

"I'd never had a home that was mine, all mine, before," she said. "It was a dream, and God had given it to me. I really appreciated it."

Gary secured a part-time job, and Tamara continued her full-time employment at the local insurance company. With her get-up-and-go personality, Tamara was able to advance in the company until she became an underwriter.

"I got pregnant and then had a miscarriage. That was very devastating to me because I desperately wanted a baby, but for some reason, I had peace about it when I lost the baby," she said.

Gary, in the meantime, went from his part-time position to a full-time permanent position. Following his first review, he was able to obtain health benefits.

After being at the insurance company for over four years, the couple made a decision that Tamara would leave and they would "try" for a baby. "I got pregnant within the first month," she said.

Fortunately, this time, she had a "great" pregnancy. "I looked good all the way through it," she said. "But then, three weeks before the baby was due, I hemorrhaged for three straight weeks. I had non-stop bleeding. We couldn't understand it. The doctors could not give me an explanation. Finally, I went into labor for four and a half days with the pains coming five minutes apart. Then they got closer and closer and I went to the hospital. I was there about five times before our baby was finally born on March 9, 1991."

For some reason, the doctor would not induce the birth no matter how much blood Tamara was losing. "I pushed for four hours and the baby would not come though I did see the crown of his head appear," said Tamara. "I believe the Lord's hand was there, keeping that baby from coming out through the birth canal. So they did a Cesarean section and he was fine."

Tamara's happiness was now complete. She had given birth to a perfectly formed son whom they called Joshua. They chose the name Joshua because it was such a strong name and it means "the Lord is salvation".

During Joshua's first year, Tamara experienced joy and peace that overwhelmed her. "I was a mother with a house paid for, two cars in the garage, a husband at work, and everything was beautiful," she recalled. "We had birthday parties and showers at the house for other people. It was just wonderful."

"I NEED THE HIV TEST"

It was nearing Joshua's first birthday. Tamara was watching a segment on an afternoon television show about the HIV virus.

"What was being said about certain people being at risk, bothered me but I tried to push it out of my mind," she recalled. "I was attending Bible studies at Calvary Chapel on Monday nights, on Tuesday evenings and on Thursday mornings. I had this wonderful life at church. I also had my lovely house where no one could get to me. So I didn't want to even consider receiving any bad news."

But the message of the television show wouldn't leave her subconscious.

"Quite suddenly, a voice rose up in my mind which said, 'Tamara, you've got to be around to take care of your son,'" she recalled. "I couldn't understand what was being said. I had started eating better, and doing exercises, but the voice wouldn't go away."

Finally, Tamara told herself, "I need an HIV test! This show has shown me that I've put myself at risk with my previous behavior patterns."

She explained, "I've always believed that you reap what you sow, and I knew that I needed some sort of medical attention. One day I called a few places that did the HIV test, but got no answer."

Gary came home one evening and casually announced that his health plan was testing for the HIV virus. "I got the number from Gary and made a call, and I got through immediately," she remembered. "I showed up for my appointment and incidentally, I had to barter with the doctor for the test. He wanted me to disclose all of my sexual past and all my drug taking."

Tamara admits to being startled that the doctor had pressed her for details of all the men she had slept with. After relenting and revealing the information, she took the test. Tamara said she felt "dirty" at having to do it.

"But one thing I knew was that Jesus Christ would never leave me nor forsake me," she said. "I was doing what He intended me to do."

A technician put a rubber tube tightly about her arm and wiped the crook of her arm with an alcohol swab. Using her teeth, she pulled the cap off the needle and inserted it into Tamara's arm. After her blood had been drawn and the technician applied a cotton ball to the puncture site, Tamara said she never gave it a second thought. "I was cocky thinking it would come up negative because I was pretty healthy," she said.

Tamara pushed to the back of her mind the fact that lately she had been suffering from fatigue. "I didn't feel up to par, but I had been breast feeding Joshua, and I felt because of this, that I couldn't expect to be a hundred percent, health-wise."

After two weeks, Tamara returned to the health clinic, but she discovered that the results hadn't yet come back from the lab.

Joshua's first birthday party came and went. "It was a wonderful time," she recalled. "There were sixty guests to share in our great happiness."

THE RESULTS

Tamara Lindley Brown jumped nervously at five o'clock one evening when an operator came on the line with an emergency breakthrough. "I was on the telephone with my mother," Tamara remembers. "I released the phone, thinking that something had happened to Gary at work. No, it was for me. It was the health clinic. The doctor stated that my test results were in, and the doctor was asking if I could 'please come in immediately.'" Tamara suddenly felt lightheaded as she tried to protest. "My baby's in the crib and my husband isn't home from work yet. I can't come in yet," she almost screamed into the phone, adding, "I will get there as quickly as I can."

The caller wouldn't tell Tamara anything over the line. "The phone spilled out of my fingers and I stumbled into the bathroom and vomited because I knew deep down what the result was," Tamara recalled.

Gary was late coming home from work that evening, so Tamara woke Joshua at five o'clock, packed him up, and started down the street in her car and saw Gary who was finally returning home. He parked his car, got in her car with her and prayed.

So, in March, 1992, Tamara faced the greatest battle of her life. The doctor was soberfaced as she came into the room at the clinic where Tamara sat in dread silence.

"Tamara," she began haltingly, "I'm afraid I have some bad news for you."

Alone in the room with her, she clasped her hands over her face in anticipation of what she was about to say.

"The test results are in and you are HIV-positive," she said, her face sad and pale, knowing she had just delivered what could be a death sentence to the beautiful young woman sitting in front of her.

Tamara was devastated. Her head began to thump and her legs suddenly felt horribly unsteady, the muscles trembling and untrustworthy. As she entered the waiting room, Gary got up from his seat and put his arms gently around his wife.

He knew what the result of the test was without a word being spoken. Not wanting Joshua to be upset, the two proud parents would not shed a tear.

"An hour later, when we got home, I lay prostrate on the floor of our house thinking that I had killed my husband and my baby," she said. "The sins of my past had come back to haunt me. I was living proof that you reap what you sow."

Both Gary and Joshua were tested for the virus, and, miraculously, both are HIV-negative.

"I was never mad at God," said Tamara, "because Jesus says in the Scriptures, '*I will never leave you or forsake you.*' I also know that '*All things work together for good....*' Even though I had been walking with the Lord for years and had not been doing anything that was dangerous for eight years, my past sins had caught up with me."

The next crisis Tamara faced was her marriage. "I told Gary that he could leave if he wished," she said. "I told him I would understand if he wanted to leave me. He was marvelous and responded by saying, 'Why would I? I married you three and a half years ago, and I would marry you again today.'"

With that, they fell into each other's arms, both of them laughing and crying at once.

Gary admits asking God at the time, "Why us? We have a beautiful house. A beautiful child. A beautiful marriage. Why do we have to go through this? What's the reason?" Gary was soon to discover the surprising reason.

The couple says they are still deeply in love and daily seek the Scriptures together for encouragement.

The next step that Tamara took was to call the men that she felt she may have put at risk through her promiscuity. "I contacted all of them and told them that I may have been a risk to them and they were tested and, fortunately, they were all negative," she said. "That was a blessing. I don't have the additional guilt about that because I did what I could by telling them."

SHUNNED BY THE CHURCH

Tamara could not believe what she was hearing. The pastor, seated before her, stated solemnly that her family was not welcome at the beloved retreat center where they had spent many previous weekends.

"We cannot stop you from coming to church, but we would prefer it if you didn't go to the retreat center," he said, pointedly.

Apparently, the pastor had a fear that being in close proximity to Tamara and her family, would scare some of the people away.

To add to the indignity, some of the friends that had attended their wedding and were at Joshua's birthday party, suddenly began to shun Gary and Tamara. "We've learned to allow them their space," she said. "They have to be responsible to the Lord with what they do. However, I don't believe I would have ever done that to someone who was suffering—whatever the reason. I'd be the first to touch them, hug them, and tell them that I cared for them and wanted to help them."

Still, not everyone ostracized them. "We still have some friends who are constantly here in our home," she said. "It is amazing. The Lord really does not leave nor forsake you in your time of trouble."

It wasn't long before Tamara discovered that her illness had an up-side. She began to give her life completely over to a new ministry. She began telling her story in local schools, colleges and universities.

"I started working in the secular world quite a bit with people like gang members, drug addicts and women in general—women who are abused ... women who are HIV infected," she said.

THE QUICKSAND OF SIN

This seemingly frail woman, now forged into tempered steel, says that the reason people listen to her is that she tells her audience, "I've been where you are! I've experienced most everything in the quicksand of sin!"

Tamara began to realize that the cast-offs from society are loved by God. "I began telling them about Jesus," she said, "...how He reached out and touched the leper."

Tamara confesses she has become "just a little tired" when some church leaders say to sinners who attend their services, "We'll allow you to continue your activity for two weeks, but in that time you had better get saved, change your life around and give yourself totally to the Lord. You will not be allowed to do anything wrong in the future."

Tamara pointed out, "These people are in bondage from a lifetime of sin. Yes, the Lord does work in mysterious ways. Sometimes His deliverance comes right away, but often it's an involvement. These people have to work through their bondage until it is slowly removed."

Gary confessed that he is "really proud of Tamara and her ministry." He stated, "She's a real servant of the Lord and works diligently in His service. I sometimes wonder where she gets all her energy, and I pray to the Lord every day that He'll give her more and more of it so she may continue her ministry. I also pray that someday the Lord will bring a cure to this terrible disease."

Tamara interjected, "As for me, I believe that God will keep me here if I have just one T-cell (the helper in the immune system) or a million. When His time limit has finally come and my days are completed in His denoted number, then I know it will be my time to go home."

Tamara remembers the day her mother was driving with her, and she looked over at her and said, "Tamara, why you? You lived out on the streets and you kicked drugs. You kicked alcohol. You worked your way up. You've become a productive citizen. You attend church. You love Jesus. Why you?"

It was a perfectly natural question for her mother to ask, but Tamara had already thought through her answer. Tamara said that her past life was a "preparedness" for her new outreach. "I don't care what people think about me because the Lord loves me," she said, "and He's never going to leave me or forsake me. He's the same yesterday, today and forever, and that's what I hold onto, Mom."

Tamara told her mother that she still makes mistakes. "I still have my bondages, and I have a bit of anger here and there, but my problems like this are coming in shorter increments of time, so I know there's a progress with Jesus."

Tamara does not feel sorry for herself, but she confesses to feeling a "righteous anger" about the way that many people with the HIV virus and AIDS are being treated by the public.

"I even feel compassion toward those ignorant people who mistreat people like myself," she said. " I want to be there for those who are being persecuted. I don't care what they've done to me. All I am aware of is that I have to keep my side of the road clean.

"I am aware that I have to do what Jesus would do. He was rejected by the people of His day. They threw him out of His own city when He went there to preach in the temple. I hang onto the Scripture which says, *'Blessed are they who are persecuted....'*"

"People have a deep fear factor of AIDS, but I know that Jesus didn't see the lepers of His day as being unclean. He didn't treat them as unclean. He reached out and touched them."

Since being shunned by some of her former friends, several of them have apologized for their actions. "There was no forgiving needed on my side," Tamara said. "They just needed time to think through what they had done to me and see that it was not in line with the teachings of Jesus Christ."

"WALK LIKE I TALK"

Tamara has also reached out to the gay community, an area shunned by many Christians who only offer judgment to these people.

"I become their friend first, and then when they see I walk like I talk, they are ready to listen to me," said Tamara. "I am against those pastors who preach that homosexuality is the 'worst sin'. These people need love and understanding like everybody else does. These judgmental pastors have alcoholics sitting in the pews, as well as food addicts—gluttony is also a sin. They are all equal in God's eyes. The Bible says that *all have sinned and fallen short of the glory of God*. I'm no better than the next because I happen to be heterosexual. If I'm heterosexual and I am into fornication, I'm into sin. If I drink too much, I'm in sin. If I eat too much and have a gluttonous obsession, I am in sin. If the exercising that you're doing becomes compulsive that also can take you away from Jesus Christ and what He has for your life. That is sin too, because you're letting that become your god. That is a false idol."

"All of the above are things we have to watch for. You cannot judge with a 'beam in your own eye'. You need to love. You have to tell people there is a Savior that loves them no matter where they have been or what they have done. The Lord can wash our sins clean. I guess I would go on sinning until the day I 'croak', but I have a Savior to help me. I tell people who are sex addicts that God will remove their bondage, but sometimes they have to do a little footwork of their own. That goes for the drug addict, the alcoholic and the food addict as well."

Tamara says that "patience is the key" to working with people with addictions. "I start by gaining their confidence and then show that I'm true, because there is a 'trust issue' with people these days," she said. "You have to show that you are trustworthy, and you are not going to leave them in the lurch. I am there to love them no matter what lifestyle they have practiced or what religion they have embraced."

Tamara says she is eternally grateful that Gary has stuck by a "woman who wears a tainted shirt for all the public to see." She calls him "a man with strong shoulders and a sympathetic ear." "That is not so for many women, including those in Christian marriages," she said. "A lot of Christian women find that once they have been diagnosed positive, their husbands leave them. These women like myself, were HIV positive because of their past, but they have been deserted in their time of need."

Gary and Tamara are approaching their fifth wedding anniversary. "We're looking forward to a beautiful time together," said Tamara. "In fact, we have been drawn closer together by this situation. What Satan could have used to build a wedge in our marriage, Jesus has turned around and used it to make us very strong. I believe because of this that we can see anything through together. We will get through the illness, as long as we walk with Jesus, and when we can't walk, we will let Him carry us."

For Tamara and Gary, marriage is definitely "for better, for worse!"

Mike Hylton

SCHOOL DAYS

1952-53

Chapter Nine

BLOOD, SWEAT AND TEARS

It was in the spring of 1947 when Mrs. Manola Mitchell Hylton bolted upright in bed at her Pulaski, Virginia home as she heard insistent crying coming from the bedroom of her one-year-old son, Mike. Wearily, she pushed aside the covers, rubbed her eyes, slid off the bed onto her feet, and went to investigate what was wrong.

She checked the clock in the bedroom. It was two o'clock in the morning. Two o'clock!

Maybe Mike's having a bad dream, she thought. A quick cuddle and a few words of encouragement would do the trick and he would drift off into uninterrupted sleep, she assured herself.

As a nurse, Mrs. Hylton was fully aware that her son was not a physically healthy child, but she was totally unprepared for what she was about to confront as she groped her way through the darkness into his room.

She switched on the light in Mike's bedroom and immediately gasped out a cry of terror as she saw blood covering the pillow and sheets of his bed.

"What's wrong, honey?" she said as she approached the terrified baby, his eyes red-rimmed from lack of sleep and his little body trembling with fear. Instantly, she remembered Mike had fallen and had bitten his tongue earlier in the day. She recalled that as long as she could keep him quiet, the bleeding would stop, but as soon as Mike began to move about, his tongue would begin to bleed again.

Mike's small face puckered woefully, etched with childhood frenzy. He was nearlyly completely covered with blood. The child began sobbing helplessly.

Mr. Vivian Hylton rolled restlessly in bed and finally sat up as the noise of the commotion shattered his sleep. He scrambled to join his wife at their son's bedside. Being a hospital administrator in Pulaski, Virginia, he had seen many terrible sights, but this was undoubtedly the worst because it involved his youngest son.

"Oh my God," he gasped. "What's wrong?"

Shivering with panic, Mrs. Hylton explained what had occurred and then turned to her husband and said resignedly, "You can't tell me that this child doesn't have a bleeding problem." The handwriting was on the wall and that disturbing thought sent a chill through both of them.

For one long year, both Mr. and Mrs. Hylton had been hoping against hope that their young son had not inherited his grandfather's bleeding disorder. After Mike was born, Mrs. Hylton had noticed bruising when she changed his diapers. She could see the dark, angry bruising around her son's ankles left there by the gentle grasping of her child's legs. When he started crawling and bruising his knees, she began to surmise that the bruising must be caused by the same disease her father had.

Now the evidence was overwhelming. Her father had died from complications of hemophilia early on in life and now it appeared that her fourth and youngest child faced this same terrible illness. The Hyltons had three sons and one daughter.

After arranging for the other three children (Buddy, Bunny, and Johnny) to stay with a neighbor, Mr. and Mrs. Hylton drove their son to the only hospital in Pulaski. There the emergency room staff worked swiftly to try and stanch the blood flow from Mike's injury. As the physician worked, the couple waited anxiously outside in a sitting room. They could not see clearly

"I pray for strength to continue Leo's work to find out what really happened so that we all will know that his death was not for naught! Leo was a board member of the Committee Of Ten Thousand 'COTT' that has been asking our FDA, our Red Cross, our pharmaceutical companies, our doctors, and many others— 'WHY?'"

Mike told me that he was not sure if Leo knew Jesus Christ as his personal Lord and Savior. "Tears come to my eyes because I'm not sure where Leo placed his faith. But as for Janet and Joe, I know they are with Jesus as we speak."

MACHINE GUN

Mike Hylton switched gears back to the blood problem. He added: "It was just like lining us up and shooting us with a machine gun with FDA approved bullets coated with the AIDS virus."

Mike discovered that his hemophilia set him apart at school. "I couldn't play sports and I had to be super careful with everything I did. If I relaxed, I paid the consequences."

He was classified as having "severe hemophilia," meaning Mike's body had less than one percent of the normal Factor VIII protein. If he had a bleeding episode, the only treatment available in his younger years was a direct blood transfusion from his father.

"I would be on one table and he'd be on another," Mike explained. "I can still see my father lying there, the doctor drawing blood from him into a syringe, turn the lever and push it into me through an intravenous needle."

This life-saving procedure took place each time Mike had a bloody nose or a hemorrhage in a knee, ankle, elbow, or basically any other joint. "If this went untreated, it created excruciating pain as the joint filled up with blood," Mike recalled. "Even if treated, the hemorrhage caused major joint damage."

In most cases, this treatment would stop the bleeding process, but eventually the medical community devised a plasma treatment that simplified the procedure.

"They'd give me the plasma which was separated from other donors' blood," he went on. "I didn't need the red blood cells unless I had lost a lot of blood. The Factor VIII protein that I needed was in the plasma."

As hemophilia research became more sophisticated, scientists developed "cryoprecipitate." "They froze the plasma and then thawed it. At a certain temperature, the Factor VIII protein would melt and they could remove it for later use in hemophilia treatment," said Mike.

"So, instead of getting one or two bags of plasma, I would get about two-hundred milliliters of cryoprecipitate which was pooled from approximately ten donors. The manufacturing process kept being refined to where it is today. I'm now using a recombinant product that is genetically made. Actually, it is not a blood product per se. The cost for this recombinant product for a single treatment is approximately $2,500."

With Mike's severe hemophilia, this treatment is necessary every five to seven days. He can treat his own hemorrhages at home or while traveling and bring his clotting level up to thirty, fifty, or even a hundred percent. "My clotting factor percentage is zero to begin with. If I take 2,000 units (20 milliliters by volume) of the recombinant clotting factor (also called 'concentrate'), I'll bring my clotting level up to between thirty and forty percent of normal. In six hours from that point, I'm at fifteen percent, six hours from that point I'm at seven-and-a-half. It has roughly a six-hour halflife," he said.

"I now have control over my treatment and within minutes can inject 'concentrate' into my system to stop a hemorrhage. Self-infusion has allowed me to experience a new freedom not only from pain but also from confinement."

During his growing-up years, Mike Hylton managed to keep relatively healthy although upon occasion, he would be rushed to a local hospital with a severe hemorrhage. Mike says you forget about pain but he was quick to recall one horrible incident while traveling to the Florida beaches during spring break in 1968. Mike recalled, "Take a twenty-four hour bus trip from Washington, D.C. to Daytona Beach, Florida; add an elbow hemorrhage somewhere near Richmond, Virginia; and you have the making of a nightmare. I had been looking forward to spending a fun-filled week in Daytona Beach and knew that I would have to be real careful not to injure myself and ruin the trip. I wasn't two hours out when I noticed my right elbow was hurting. The cushioned arm rest on my seat was gone and bare metal became the secret enemy.

"I wasn't going to get off the bus to find a hospital somewhere and spend my vacation trying to explain to the on-call doctor what was wrong and what I needed. I had been through that routine before. I had also been in pain many times before but being confined on a crowded bus trying to not hurt, was pure 'hell.' The hours at night were the worst. I remember moving to the far back of the bus, finding a corner, and silently crying the miles away.

"Somewhere in Georgia at one of the multitude of bus stops along the way, I called my brother who was waiting for me in Florida," Mike said. "I gave John my arrival schedule, phone numbers of my doctors who were 1,000 miles away but knew what to do, and told John to contact a local hospital. I needed to have him 'work it out' so that I received immediate treatment upon arrival. John knew I was in no condition to get caught up in 'the system.'"

"Thank God, I spent only four days in bed. I even managed to get a whopper of a sunburn to take back to college for bragging rights," he said.

FIRST LOVES

Mike Hylton was born in the small Virginia town of Pulaski on July 29, 1946. As a child growing up, Mike's fondest memories are of living in a large house in Inwood, West Virginia, situated next to an active farm with dairy cattle, pigs, chickens, horses, and everything else that goes with farming. During the summers, Mike spent many hours driving the "gigantic" farm tractor as the neighboring farmer and his wife threw bails of hay onto the trailing hay wagon. At the young age of eight, all Mike had to do was to steer the giant tractor and ease his foot off the clutch ever so gently to move the hay wagon forward at a slow enough speed so that the farmers could do their jobs. "I can still see and hear Isabel Dick screaming and laughing at me while trying to keep her balance on top of the hay when I popped the clutch too fast and the tractor lurched forward," Mike recalled. "I grew up on that farm and I must say those were the happiest days of my childhood. Burley and Isabel wouldn't let me do any real physical work around the farm but they always made me feel that I was someone special."

Mike decided to level with Sharon Fulk, his high school sweetheart. "By the age of forty, I'll be in a wheelchair," he told her one day. "I want you to know this because I would like you to become my wife."

The couple had first met in chemistry class at the local high school in Martinsburg, West Virginia.

"I was always a kind of shy fellow," Mike admitted. "Because of this, I didn't date much in high school. Whenever I had a 'bleed' in my knee, ankle, or elbow, I would turn up in class with my arm in a sling or on crutches."

"Bill Kogelschatz, a mutual friend, took it upon himself to try and bring Sharon and me together. Bill sat between us in chemistry class, and he would pass notes or make comments. We had one chemistry instructor who was really an odd fellow. He decided that I was disrupting the class. His punishment was to bring me up front, sit me on a stool in the corner, and humiliate me. So, I met my wife by being shamed in front of the class. I think she felt sorry for me."

Considering Mike's hemophilia condition, their first date was entirely unexpected. "We climbed a mountain in Harper's Ferry, West Virginia, overlooking the junction of the Shenandoah and Potomac Rivers which was a feat in itself because I was just coming off a knee hemorrhage at the time," Mike stated.

Sadly, the romance broke up in 1963 when Mike moved to the Washington D.C. area. Mike finished high school, attended a community college and acquired a degree in computer science. While he was studying in the nation's capital, Sharon attended Shepherd College in Shepherdstown, West Virginia.

"Fortunately, we got back together again and I proposed to her at the Candlelight Restaurant in Martinsburg," he recalled. "We talked about my hemophilia and what it meant to our future. Sharon was aware of the implications of marrying me. She knew because of the genetic condition, any daughter we might have would be a carrier.

"We had very good communication regarding life in general. We were in love and hemophilia was just another element of our relationship."

CHOICES

Mike had been living with his parents in Silver Spring, Maryland, when the couple was married in Martinsburg, West Virginia on April, 5, 1969. They spent their honeymoon at

Virginia Beach. "Our honeymoon was special. We were in love and we both were virgins by choice. I've talked to many kids and adults regarding HIV, AIDS, sexual abstinence and choices they must make. Many people seem to believe that sexual activity prior to marriage is acceptable—kind of like trying out the merchandise before you buy. But take it from two people who waited, sex is not the fundamental component of a relationship. Love, commitment—and most importantly, God are the keys to a great relationship.

"For us, there was no merchandise, there were two people in love wanting more than anything not to hurt the other. Staying a virgin during the 1960's was a miracle in itself," Mike continued. "Although I wasn't thinking about or seeking God at that time, God never lost sight of me. Looking back, I see many times that God carried me through valleys where I surely would have fallen away had I been alone. We're glad we waited and God has honored this decision in our marriage and in our walk with Jesus Christ."

Mike continued: "We were married two months before Sharon finished her senior year at college," he said. "She graduated with a degree in education and we moved into an apartment in Rockville, Maryland. Sharon started teaching that fall at Parkland Junior High School in Rockville."

It appeared to both of them in these early days of wedded bliss that a wonderful life lay ahead of them, but that turned out to be an illusion.

Chapter Ten

GO WEST, YOUNG MAN

Perspiration beaded Mike's brow and his strained face turned a fire-engine red color.

"Are you all right, honey?" Sharon anxiously asked her husband of a few weeks. She had just arrived home from attending classes seventy-five miles away.

"No, I feel terrible," Mike spoke in a whisper, his speech breathless. "I've hurt my shoulder somehow and the pain is so bad I can hardly stand it. The pain pills haven't worked. I've been waiting for you."

Only too aware that her husband was in serious trouble, Sharon immediately called his doctor and drove Mike to the National Institute of Health (NIH) in Bethesda, Maryland. Mike was a "regular" at NIH because he had been involved in their research into hemophilia since he was eleven years old. She knew he would get immediate attention there. Sharon recalled that Mike was in so much discomfort that she had to stop the car along the way numerous times so that he could get out and move around in an attempt to relieve some of the pain.

When they arrived, Mike was exhausted and groggy from the pain medication he had taken at home. Sharon cautiously helped Mike as he stumbled unsteadily toward the transfusion treatment room. There, the NIH staff was waiting with the blood he needed to stop the hemorrhage. Mike received immediate care. With the hemorrhage stopped, only time and rest would reduce the fluid in his swollen shoulder and relieve the pain. The doctor on call wanted to admit his half-conscious patient into the hospital. He was still in agonizing pain, but Mike knew he would be more comfortable at home once the pain started to decrease in intensity.

After a shot of Demerol and a two-hour restless, sleep-like trance at the Medical Center, Sharon returned home with her husband. They did not speak on the way since Mike was still dazed from all the medication. Sharon was trying to assess the seriousness of what had just happened. For Sharon, this was just a foretaste of what was to lie ahead.

Over the next few years, Mike was able to secure a succession of computer jobs. "When I was in college, I did an internship with Associated Mortgage Company in Washington, D.C. as a computer operator and programmer. After graduation, I became a programmer/analyst with the firm," he recalled. "I thought I had the world by the tail, but I was too immature in the ways of the business world to fully understand what they meant by 'responsibility and commitment'. In fact, I had a real attitude problem and eventually I was fired. I still marvel at knowing that we tend to learn more from our mistakes than we do from our accomplishments. Looking back, I should have been fired months before they actually let me go.

"The next company I went to work for was called DataMedics, Inc. I was the programmer/analyst in a small medical billing firm. In fact, I was kind of the jack of all trades (account representative, computer operator, programmer, analyst, and courier)."

TWICE BORN

It seemed that the couple was meant to stay in Maryland for the rest of their lives, but God had other plans. While working with DataMedics, Mike spotted an advertisement in the Washington Post for a computer expert. It had been placed by a large engineering and construction firm in San Francisco. The company was looking for someone with his particular computer skills to work at a local Maryland office. He sent in his resume and waited for their response. It wasn't long in coming.

The interview took place at Bechtel Power Corporation's Maryland office in the aftermath of Hurricane Agnes which had devastated much of the East Coast in early 1972. "I remember driving to the interview through terrible flooding," he recalled. Darrel Snider seemed impressed with Mike's skills and awarded him the job. He began a slow climb up the company ladder.

God had not figured much in Mike Hylton's life up to that time. After all, Mike was a survivor with a life-threatening illness that would only get worse as the years passed. Still, a dramatic change lay ahead for him. It began during a business trip to Bechtel's home office in San Francisco. After his meetings, he flew down to the Los Angeles area to visit with his brother, John. John had been a pilot with TransWorld Airlines and was now an associate pastor at Calvary Chapel in Costa Mesa under Chuck Smith's leadership.

"John was converted to Christianity during the days of the Jesus Movement and (without my knowledge) had spent many years praying for me," Mike revealed. "He is an incredibly talented and gifted man who led the Wednesday night worship service at Calvary Chapel. He had also been a singer with the New Christy Minstrels."

During his stay at John's Costa Mesa home, Mike attended a potluck dinner with John, his wife, Mary Ann, and seven other couples from Calvary Chapel.

"They appeared to be very nice people but they really 'worked on me' that night," Michael recalled. "They decided that it was time that Mike met Jesus Christ, but I resisted their efforts with every fiber of my mind and body."

As different people talked to Mike about surrendering his life to Jesus Christ, he couldn't comprehend what they were talking about.

"I had experienced no problem in praying," he said. "I'd always believed in God and I was sure that there was this man known as Jesus Christ who was the Son of God."

Sitting on a sofa that Saturday night twenty years ago, Mike Hylton shared his personal ideas on faith with those that were challenging him. One of the group then said pointedly, "Mike, you know, Satan believes that too. You're so close, but there's another dimension that you have to understand. Your salvation is wrapped up in it."

It seemed to Mike that at the moment, almost everyone in the room was gunning for his soul. "However, I wasn't intimidated or threatened," he recalled. "I could see that what they were saying was something they believed with real zest."

Mike began to notice tears on some of the ladies' faces who were watching the drama unravel. "They were standing in the background, and it suddenly hit me that they were silently praying for this lost sinner," he recalled. Mike, however, continued to rebut all that was said to him. "Still, I didn't sleep much that night," he remembers.

The following day, John drove his brother to the airport for his return flight to Maryland. As they cruised along on the San Diego Freeway toward Los Angeles International Airport, John was gripping the steering wheel tightly, and said, "Mike, you really have to know the truth. You need to understand who Jesus Christ is—that He is your Lord and Savior and He died on the cross for you. He loves you."

Mike recalled that his brother's words echoed in the recesses of his brain and sounded like "Blah-blah, blah-blah, blah-blah. Pound, pound, pound. Beat, beat, beat." In spite of that, Mike was hearing a small voice that was speaking to him from somewhere.

When John finally paused for breath, Mike said firmly, "John, if you would just shut up, I'd like to accept Jesus into my heart."

John was speechless and nearly swerved with excitement. "This was somewhere on the freeway between Costa Mesa and LAX," recalled Mike. "He pulled over and, as the traffic roared by, I prayed and asked Jesus Christ into my life."

As his brother prayed, John could not hold back the tears that welled up in his eyes.

"Not a day has passed since then that I didn't know that there was a change in me," said Mike.

When he returned home, Mike shared with Sharon what had happened to him. "She was not a Christian at the time, but she could see that there was something different about me," he said.

Sharon's time to surrender her life to Jesus Christ came a few months later during a visit to Redding, California, where John had moved. John casually asked Sharon one day, "How long have you been a Christian?"

Sharon responded by saying, "I'm not! I've been involved in a home Bible study and everyone thinks I'm a Christian but I know that I have never invited Jesus into my heart."

John then pressed her. "Well, do you want to?" he asked.

"Yes," she replied. So with that, John prayed with her and she too became a born-again Christian.

Mike and Sharon started attending a church in Frederick, Maryland that their next-door neighbors, Nan and Ken Walker attended. There were ten couples that formed a home fellowship group. Over the years, this group has remained a spiritual influence in their lives. They still keep close contact with yearly visits and frequent correspondence. This mighty prayer group is only a phone call away. All of the women in the group also belonged to Community Bible Study, an international Bible study and ministry for women. During the difficult years to come, Sharon's involvement in "CBS" would provide major spiritual support for the entire family.

WESTWARD LEADING

In 1981, Mike and Sharon felt a "leading of the Lord" and Mike transferred to the Los Angeles division of Bechtel Power Corporation. He had started in Maryland as a programmer/analyst and had worked his way into a position as programming supervisor. Upon his transfer to Los Angeles, Mike became the programming manager there.

"In the interim, Courtney, our daughter, was born in 1975," said Mike. "In 1978, Sean was born. We spaced the children three years apart on purpose. About a year later we got a surprise; Sharon was again pregnant. Our second son, Todd, was born nineteen months after Sean. We now had three beautiful children."

As Mike's hemophilia condition gradually worsened, he underwent a series of tricky orthopedic operations.

"I had both my knees replaced because of hemophilia arthropathy," he said. "If you have one hemorrhage in a joint, the fluid causes degenerative changes. I've had hundreds of hemorrhages and consequently the joints became so damaged that both my knees have had to be replaced."

"During the recovery of my first knee replacement surgery, I experienced what I'd call one of my first answers to prayer," Mike said. Mike tolerated the surgery well but had been running a fever for a few days. It was obvious that there was some infection that his body was fighting off and the fever was weakening him. About the third evening, Mike called Sharon and said, "I'm in trouble and I need help. Call your Community Bible Study prayer line and start the prayer chain going. I can't take much more of this!" By morning, Mike's fever had broken. Was this an answer to prayer? "No question in my mind." Was this a miracle? Mike says, "No question in my mind about that, either.

"I've also had terrible problems with my ankles and at one time, I was almost totally crippled. They can't replace ankles, so both of them have been fused. I've had numerous operations on my elbows. The doctors were going to operate on my right elbow again when I got really sick in 1991. They were also going to replace my right shoulder with a ball and socket and re-fuse my right ankle because I had broken a metal pin in it. My doctors and I finally decided against the operations. The way things were going, it appeared that I would end up in a wheelchair as I had predicted." Mike couldn't use crutches because his arms, elbows and shoulders were so damaged.

Like all hemophiliacs, Michael has endured the problems with internal bleeding in his joints. "That's the major difficulty," he explained. "We don't bleed to death from cutting ourselves while shaving as many people seem to think."

Still, he is not bitter with the cross he has had to bear. "I would say, I've really been blessed from day one," he said surprisingly. "I have had to deal with a lot of physical pain and limitations, but there have been so many blessings that they take precedence over everything I've been through."

The transition of moving from Maryland to Southern California was difficult for the family, but still they found a warm fellowship at Calvary Chapel. God was becoming "priority number one" in their lives. "Each of the children has subsequently professed a knowledge and an acceptance of Jesus as their personal Savior," Mike added proudly.

One by one, they have been saved. Mike says that when he thinks of his brother John who baptized Sharon, Courtney, and Sean, he is reminded of the song, "*Thank You*" by Ray Boltz. Mike continues to give constant thanks to God for his brother's faithfulness in his prayer life and witness to Mike's family.

"I look at all the people my brother has touched in and through my life and probably thousands of other people, and when I hear that song, I see him in my mind's eye. I think, *'Wouldn't that be great if that's how John was treated when he makes it to heaven?'* I can picture the Lord taking hold of John's arm, and saying, 'Great is your reward. Look at all the lives that you touched.'"

Even so, Mike Hylton admits that it wasn't until 1991 that he fully turned his life unreservedly over to Jesus Christ.

"I almost died from complications of my medical condition," he said. "Prior to 1991, I would walk up to a door, an opportunity, and I had the Scripture to help me. I knew how to wait on the Lord, and I had a foundation in the Christian faith. It came about long after I was a Christian, no question about it, but I really wasn't seeking the Lord's direction for my life. Many of the things that I did, I'm sure the Lord just honored and blessed, but it was me who decided to do them."

"The analogy that I use is that I'd walk up to those doors and consciously pray, 'Lord, which one do you want me to walk through? Door number one? Door number two? Door number three?'" Mike stated that he would step out in faith, and "put my shoulder up against door number two, push it open, and think, 'Maybe there's an opportunity there, a blessing, whatever.' But it was all me doing it."

ANOTHER MIRACLE

A "reality check" in Mike Hylton's spiritual walk came in 1991 while he was playing table tennis (Ping-Pong) with another couple during a party in Garden Grove.

"I had a cast on my right leg because I was having ankle difficulty, and I was back-pedaling to catch my balance. I fell against a block wall and cracked my head," Mike said. "Everybody, even the kids in the swimming pool underwater, heard it. I should have died."

Mike believes his life was saved because some of the Christians at the party saw him back-pedaling, and they were already praying for him before he hit the wall.

"The worst injury that a person with hemophilia can sustain is a head injury," he recalled. "I blacked out for a second or so and struggled to maintain consciousness."

He was rushed home, took his injection of antihemophilic factor, and was driven to the emergency room of Hoag Hospital in Newport Beach to have a CAT scan of his head. "Miraculously, they found no damage," he said. "I had a little headache, and that was all. The incident was a miracle in itself. The only way I can explain it is that protection occurred because of prayer of those who witnessed the accident. An instant healing had taken place or the hand of the Lord cushioned my fall."

Chapter Eleven

"MIKE, YOU'VE GOT AIDS"

The doctor's passing comment didn't really hit home with Mike Hylton at the time it was made.

"We don't know what that means," said the white-coated physician, allowing her hand to touch Mike's arm, "but there are people, mostly gay men, dying out there of strange diseases and infections. We have discovered that their T-cells are affected, and I did a T-cell count on you and there is no question, Mr. Hylton, that your T-cells are affected."

Mike looked puzzled. "What do you mean that my T-cells are affected?" he asked.

"We don't know," admitted the doctor. "All I can tell you is that there is some chance that the blood products you have received for your hemophilia may have been contaminated."

As a board member of the Southern California Hemophilia Foundation, Mike Hylton had been following the harrowing story of how the blood supply had been corrupted resulting in thousands of hemophiliacs around the world contracting the AIDS virus. But surely, now he was a Christian, this could not happen to him!

It was 1985 before the shocking truth was finally understood by both the doctor and by Mike Hylton.

THE HIV TEST

During a routine visit, Mike's doctor suggested that he take an HIV test.

"We've seen so many hemophiliacs develop AIDS or whatever this disease is," she said almost reflectively. "Your blood shows a change. We still don't know for sure what it means, but we do know that men who are dying of AIDS have a change in their blood which results in the lowering of their T-4 and T-8 counts and the ratio between the two reverses."

Mike took the test by which the medical laboratory could measure whether or not HIV antibodies had developed in his bloodstream. He returned a few days later for the results. They were not good!

"Mike, we've suspected this for a long time and I know it's not going to come as a shock to you," the doctor began hesitantly, "so I won't beat about the bush. I'm sorry to tell you that you've been infected with the AIDS virus."

"What?" responded Mike, taking a deep breath and then letting it out slowly. Time seemed to stop for Mike and he could only repeat, "What!?"

"Mike, you've got AIDS!" said the physician, her normally composed face flushed.

Mike Hylton shook his head in disbelief. It was as though a knife had pierced his heart. He tried to speak, but nothing came out of his mouth. The small exam room they sat in seemed to grow dark and cold.

Mike was all alone on the two-hour drive home from that downtown Los Angeles hospital. After gathering his whirling thoughts, the next step was to tell Sharon the terrible news. Sharon was stunned, but the reality that Mike was infected was mostly a confirmation of something they both had suspected. Mike asked Sharon to take the HIV test. The results came back negative. God's grace was again realized.

Like almost everyone who has been told they are HIV positive, Mike Hylton went through a process of denial. "It didn't make any sense," he recalled, "I knew—but I didn't know. My 'denial' was to keep on going as if nothing were wrong. I had fought hemophilia for so long that this new 'deal of the cards' was just another annoyance. It wasn't until about four years later when my T-cells dropped below 200 that I finally had to stop pretending that another life threatening disease was not affecting me. Reality set in when I finally understood and accepted that this disease had the potential to infect my best friend, my wife! At this point," Mike recalled, "Sharon and I started to face this new problem head on."

Surely things couldn't get any worse. Well, they could and they did!

The next piece of bad news that came was that he had to retire from his job in late 1985 because of his hemophilia, fatigue, and generally failing health. "I took medical disability leave after my second knee replacement and after finding out that I was HIV positive," Mike explained. "I could have retired because of the hemophilia prior to 1985, but I kept going. Finally, I knew I didn't have the strength or energy to continue with my work. Unknown to me at the time, my biggest problem, fatigue, was HIV related. I battled it for a time, but it finally overwhelmed me."

ROCK BOTTOM

The day that Mike Hylton finally hit rock bottom—physically, emotionally and spiritually—was June 20, 1991.

"I had been getting progressively weaker, and I started telling my doctors about this fact," he remembered.

With each passing day, Mike Hylton was becoming weaker and the two-year slide apparently couldn't be reversed. "By February of 1991, I had gotten so weak that I could not even get up out of bed or out of a chair without help," he recalled. "I could not even turn the key in the ignition of my car or open the refrigerator door at home. I didn't have enough strength in my hand to hold the handle and pull it."

As Mike lay in bed getting weaker by the minute, he couldn't even lift his head up off the pillow and on occasions when he tried to walk, he would stumble and fall to the ground. It didn't appear that Mike Hylton's body could take much more.

As the final strength began to ebb from his body, Mike got Sharon to phone his doctor and then hold the receiver as he explained on the phone, "Doc, I've got some big problems here."

For Mike Hylton to acknowledge this was enough for his new physician, Dr. Logan. When he heard Mike's description of what was happening to him, the doctor immediately called ahead and had him admitted to Huntington Memorial Hospital in Pasadena on April 30, 1991.

"There they diagnosed that I also had polymyositis, a muscle inflammation, and they put me on steroids," Mike recalled. "The new medication damaged the pancreas quickly, further complicating things by causing diabetes, glaucoma, and cataracts.

"They started an immunoadsorption procedure, which is like dialysis. They put me on diabetic oral medication, but that didn't work. When I started insulin injections three times a day, things began to stabilize, but this new disease of polymyositis still continued." During this time, Mike lost over sixty pounds. His whole body shook physically as a reaction to the high dose of Prednisone being administered. It was later determined that Mike was battling Hepatitis A during that time, too.

BLACK THURSDAY

Everything came crashing down on June 20th, 1991—"Black Thursday" as Mike named that fateful day. He looked so ill that his eyes had sunk into their sockets and were surrounded by circles so dark he looked like he had black eyes.

"I had been released from the hospital to my Costa Mesa home and I was feeling extremely fatigued," he said. "I had been getting my dialysis-type treatments at the Huntington Hospital Hemophilia Treatment Center in Pasadena, but because of my condition, I found I couldn't cope with the one-hundred-mile commute twice a week. So I changed my doctors to down here in Orange County to handle my HIV and polymyositis."

When Mike moved his medical care, a new set of circumstances evolved with his insurance company. "New doctors had to be authorized and checked out, and the insurance company stated, 'We won't continue to pay for the treatments that Mr. Hylton is having.'"

Mike received this news on Black Thursday. "I'd been experiencing a continuing decrease in strength and I had already informed my doctors that I felt I only had three months to live unless things reversed themselves," he said. "I didn't think I would survive past August."

With death approaching, Mike began his preparation for dying by updating his will and putting everything in order. "I was dying, there was no question about it," he said. "And it was on Black Thursday that I finally lost all hope."

On June 20th, Mike called his brother, John, and told him, "I've got to see you and talk to you. John, sensing a real crisis, canceled a lunch appointment he had scheduled with a client and we met for lunch at a restaurant near John Wayne Airport." It was then that Mike broke down. "I had no control over my emotions," he remembers. "I had no control over my life at this point. I still believed in God, but I had lost all hope and I was dying. As far as I was concerned, I was already dead."

It turned out that Black Thursday really wasn't "black" after all for John told his brother that he needed to take another step of faith and completely hand his life over to Jesus Christ.

"When I returned home," Mike said, "I began to pray, 'Lord, that's it, I can't cope any more. I can't do it. I'm dying. I'm Yours. Do with me what You wish.'"

VICTORY THURSDAY

"I never lost my faith, but I had lost hope. Still, the Lord honored my faith. From that point on, my life changed. Miracles of healing began. Then I heard the still, small voice of the Lord which I had come to recognize, telling me, 'Mike, that wasn't Black Thursday, buddy. That was **Victory Thursday** for you.'"

John had become a practicing attorney and had met an evangelistic couple from Garden Grove named Ralph and Lorine Curlee. This loving couple held a Bible study in their home. "They had been praying for a Christian attorney to handle a legal matter when God directed them to John," explained Mike.

After being with his distraught brother in the restaurant, John went to meet with Ralph and Lorine. Sensing a problem, they asked John if they could help him. When they heard about Mike's desperate situation, they began fervent prayer and fasting, and started a prayer chain for Mike that continues today.

"They also put my name on all kinds of prayer lists all over the country," recalled Mike. "By the following Monday, I already had a new lease on life. I sensed a change even in that short time. For me to be where I was on that Thursday (a point of no hope), and then by Monday all of a sudden to see a change, an increase in strength which I had not seen in a period of approximately three years, was a miracle."

AGAINST ALL HOPE

"This wonderful couple, whom I still had not met, through their faith and prayers, had helped me to restore my 'Hope For Tomorrow.'" When Mike eventually got together with them, he discovered that "these people were filled with faith."

One day, Mike attended the Curlee's Bible study and the attendees gathered around Mike and began to pray for him. "I received an inner healing of the soul which was tremendous. I no longer had to wonder, 'Why do I have hemophilia? Why do I have HIV?' I was 'spiritually healed' from everything,'" he stated. "I could accept it all from the hand of my loving Savior."

Sharon says that a highlight of their life together was seeing what happened to her husband since Victory Thursday. Sharon recalled the transition. "He didn't climb out of that black hole of despair, he was lifted out," she said. "It was absolutely amazing. He's always had a lot of faith, but I can't even begin to touch the faith that he now has. I am so pleased to see the way he's handling things and to know that it's because of his faith. It is really an ongoing thing.

"It's not a plateau. I see him involved in so many different things, and each project is constantly building his faith too," Sharon added.

Mike Hylton decided that he would fight his insurance company's denial of his treatment. "Each apheresis procedure cost approximately $3,000," he said. "My blood is withdrawn and the plasma is separated from the red cells. The plasma is directed through a special column made by Imre Corporation where they extract the antibodies that are destructive, that are running amuck, and then everything is given back to me," he explained. "The procedure takes over three hours. On the following day, I received 25 grams of gamma globulin over a four-hour time period. The gamma globulin and its administration cost approximately $2,000 and was prescribed to 'jump-start' my immune system. I won the battle with my insurance company and have had well over seventy of these procedures to keep me alive."

Mike paused when he told me this and then added, "My faith and hope are fighting all my illnesses and keeping me alive. The Holy Spirit that lives within me has told me, 'Mike, you're worth it. The doctors and the pills aren't keeping you alive. It's just God.'

"When the Lord wants to take me home, I'll go home. I am to do what I can and believe that the doctors and the pills and the procedures and the different people that I run into as a result of this are part of the overall picture."

To help fight the progression of the virus' attack on his body, Mike has taken AZT, ddI, ddC, and even the experimental medication called d4T. Each of these has had to be discontinued as drug complications began to appear. Mike showed me a list of approximately twenty drugs he is currently taking. With all this medication, he jokingly refers to his body as a "toxic waste dump", but knows his body is really the temple of the Holy Spirit.

During this period, Sharon projected a great deal of strength. "She is not an emotional-type person," he said. "This was during a time when we were keeping all of this a secret, too. No one knew that I was HIV positive. Neither of us had been getting support from our friends or our church. We had not told them of the problems because we feared that the church and maybe even some of our friends would not understand. We feared the support we so desperately needed would not be available. In particular, we feared rejection.

"I think it was hardest on Sharon and the children to see what I was going through physically and emotionally. Like probably everyone with some serious or terminal illness, I've been depressed enough times to have considered ending my life. The thought of suicide, however, is not an option. It might be the 'easy way out' but the repercussions on the loved ones left behind are so far-reaching as to make this option null and void.

"Regarding suicide, I shudder to think that one of my children, my wife, a family member, or a friend might feel some guilt in their mind during a passing notion of, 'If I had only done more or said something different ....' Furthermore, God doesn't need my help —when He's ready to take me home, He will. When I surrendered all to the Lord, I became an open book to everyone. God is in control and I have turned my life and my family over to God."

A WALKING MEDICAL ENCYCLOPEDIA

Mike has become a walking medical encyclopedia. "Besides being diagnosed with hemophilia, polymyositis, hepatitis A, B and C, hypertension, diabetes, HIV, AIDS, cataracts and glaucoma, I was recently diagnosed with hypothyroidism," he said. "In addition, the doctors say I have liver disease, pancreatitis, peripheral neuropathy, constant ringing in my ears, and athlete's foot." He laughed as he ended his list with the last two problems. "Otherwise," Mike continued, "I'm in pretty good shape."

He says he is reminded how well God made the human body, and how much the human body really can go through. "I know that the Lord is not going to burden us more than what we can tolerate," he said.

HOPE FOR TOMORROW

As Mike Hylton began to pick up the threads of his life again, he remembered the time he rented a single-engine plane and flew over the area where he lived in Maryland. As he watched the houses and the fields pass below, he suddenly saw the word "HOPE" etched in the grass of someone's yard. Mike's heart leapt as he read it. As the plane got close to the field where he was to land, he said to himself, "HOPE! I think that's what I'll adopt as my middle name."

After a safe touchdown, he drove back to his home and began sketching a logo with the words, "Hope For Tomorrow." The logo was completed many years later with the help of Dan Newmire, a Christian artist. Mike explained, "The logo is a flaming torch with a red blooddrop representing life, hemophilia, and the blood of Christ. Flowing into the blood is the word 'Hope' and the words 'For Tomorrow' form the base." Mike added ,"I would say that even before I knew Jesus Christ as my personal savior, 'HOPE' was etched in my heart."

It wasn't long after this that Mike was able to put his new HOPE into action. Mike related that he bought a house in Maryland with a half-acre lot in the back of the house.

"One Saturday morning it was hot, humid, and the grass was two feet tall. I had a big, riding Ford mower," he recalled. "I got the thing out and drove into the back yard. As I looked at the task in front of me, I realized that the grass was too thick for me to mow. So I drove to the middle of the grass field, lowered the blade, and spelled out the word HOPE. Then I lifted the blade of the mower, took it back and parked it in the garage. The word HOPE has stayed with me as a gift from God even though I didn't understand it at that time. I don't know who may have seen this word from an airplane but I'm sure God had someone else needing the message I wrote in the field."

Even though that particular day he wasn't able to cut the grass, he knew that one day he would complete the task. After all, with the middle name HOPE, Mike Hylton should be able to do anything even if the situation looks absolutely—HOPELESS!

Chapter Twelve

HE INTENDS VICTORY

In many ways, it was not surprising to discover that Mike Hylton suffered from what the world calls homophobia (a fear and disgust of homosexuals). This feeling may have been enhanced since it was probably a gay man ... or gay men, who passed the AIDS virus on to him through the tainted blood supply.

One day, however, God convicted Mike of his long-lasting hostility after he made a sarcastic remark to Herb Hall during a get-together at The Village Church of Irvine.

"I pulled him aside and said, 'Herb, I made a comment recently that really bothered me.'" Mike confessed to feeling a sudden spasm of remorse.

"Herb, being a true friend, had not responded to my 'gay' joke, but it concerned me that I had offended this dear man. So I asked him to forgive me and to tell me in the future when I said hurtful things that I shouldn't have said. It was then that God reminded me that I constantly tend to make jokes that can really hurt people."

Mike first met Herb Hall after becoming involved in a hemophilia support group for those who are HIV positive and one of the participants spoke of a man named Herb. At these meetings, Mike always shared his "Hope For Tomorrow" slogan with all who were there. "When I committed my life completely to Jesus Christ, I began using it all the time," he explained. "With every organization I got involved with, I felt the Holy Spirit directing me to tell them exactly where I was coming from. I would tell them that we have left God out of our lives too long. I would say that my faith and hope are in Jesus Christ. I believe that there is going to be a cure, but it's not going to come from a Doctor Salk. A Doctor Salk may eventually get the credit for it, but I would say that the cure will come directly from God."

At one of the hemophilia/HIV support groups, Mike met Philip, a twenty-two-year-old man who was dying of AIDS dementia.

"To witness someone going through this is very saddening," said Mike. "The best thing I can say is that Phil really didn't know what was happening to him."

The next meeting was in Mike's home and he got into an intense discussion with Phil about homosexuality. "There is nothing wrong with homosexuality," Phil once again asserted haughtily, leering full into Mike's friendly eyes and giving a little defensive laugh. This comment always caused Mike's hackles to rise. A wrinkle of consternation passed over Mike's face. As in previous discussions and after a few moments of eye contact, Mike asked Phil brusquely, "What is sin? If there is nothing wrong with it, what is right and what is wrong? What is the basis of your judgment?" Mike's face had a flush on it and his eyes were throwing sparks in every direction.

Mike's brow darkened as he explained, "Phil was very dogmatic and opinionated, and since I didn't have this group under prayer, I didn't seem to have the Holy Spirit guiding me. I just had me. It was all me. To those watching it was like they were witnessing some apocalyptic tennis match. But later I forgot this raw power struggle after God showed me that He had put me there to be a witness." Mike added, "I wasn't there by accident."

Phil was not gay and apparently enjoyed stirring up Mike with his comments. Mike again opined, "Homosexuality is sin like adultery is sin ... like cheating on your income taxes is sin." Mike tried to explain that sin was part of our nature and that he wasn't passing judgment on people, only on their actions. Mike was naming 'sin' basing his judgment on the Bible teaching. Phil wouldn't let go of his assertion, but neither would Mike back off from his view. Suddenly, Phil switched topics to his friend, Herb Hall, whom he had met at another support group.

"You could say that this was Phil's way of diverting the conversation," recalled Mike. "But I know it was the method the Lord used to confirm that I needed to take this group under prayer."

Mike sees irony in the fact that it took a non-believer to make the connection between Herb and himself. "In the process, I subsequently took Phil to the believers' meeting at the Curlee's where he accepted the Lord," said Mike. "Phil is now with the Lord."

Back to the get-together in Mike's home. "Phil had talked about Herb saying that he viewed him as a 'religious fanatic,'" said Mike.

He told Phil, "The next time you talk to Herb, please give him my phone number and ask him to call me." Shortly afterwards, Herb called Mike at home and they talked for over two hours.

"It was incredible," recalled Mike. "Our hearts, our calling, our desires, the voice of the Spirit were so in tune that I realized we hadn't met by accident."

Mike was shocked when Herb suddenly revealed that he had come out of the gay lifestyle. Mike had such an aversion to people who were, or had been homosexual, and yet he warmed to Herb who seemed such a sincere person.

"Herb called me a couple of days before his very first HIV support group meeting at the Crystal Cathedral," said Mike. "He told me that he was with an organization called Naaman's Fellowship that was working with HIV-positive people." Herb and Mike shared the understanding that their meeting was not by chance—it was planned by God.

Some time during the following months, Herb asked Mike to consider joining the board of directors of Naaman's Fellowship. Mike sought the Lord on this, but felt God was telling him, "Mike, you're not to be on the board of Naaman's. I want you to support Herb as a person."

Mike explained, "Here was a man who was so gifted, so blessed and the Lord put us together for some reason. God told me that He wanted me to be Herb's 'Silas' like in Acts 15:40. I keep reminding myself of this relationship. I met Herb because of a miracle through a non-believer, and the Lord has called me to be a counsel for Herb, a support, somebody he can go to, somebody he can cry with, somebody he can laugh with. However, the Lord may have given Herb to me as well for he is somebody that I can laugh and cry with."

HOMOPHOBIA

Mike remembers vividly when his homophobia finally left him. "I was in St. Louis at a MANN training conference. MANN stands for the Men's Advocacy Network of the National Hemophilia Foundation." He recalled, "There was Steve, a young fellow about twenty whom I had noticed squirreling around. He introduced himself to the room of peers gathered together from our region of the United States. He explained that he had hemophilia with an inhibitor. An inhibitor is something that keeps the medication that is to stop bleeding from working. Your body recognizes it as a foreign substance and destroys it." Steve also said that he was gay.

"Normally the hair on my arms would have stood up," said Mike. "Earlier when I had introduced myself to the group, I shared my faith with them. I introduced myself saying that God is the power that keeps me going. When it came to Steve and he told us of his background, I felt a deep compassion for him. At that moment, the Lord took my homophobia away. I felt God telling me, 'Mike, I love this man as much as I love you.'"

Mike Hylton was taken aback and his jaw dropped in unfeigned surprise. The man was gay and yet the Lord was telling him that He loved him very much. Mike said his only concept of homosexuals, until then, was the repulsion he felt of imagining two men having sex. Now he saw that God loved the gay person and wanted to save and deliver that individual, as He does all sinners.

As Mike contemplated his homophobia, he felt God had reprimanded him by saying, "Mike, can't you see that you've been blinded by not understanding My ability to love. You blinded yourself but it's time to 'see' Who I really am."

Mike Hylton began to feel that the Lord wanted him to carry a message to everyone who would listen. He describes the message he received from God as, "Go into the churches and the HIV community. Pray constantly and love, support, and educate people. Concentrate on those that are ripe for picking and don't beat your head against the wall of a heart that I may have already hardened."

Mike began to try to reflect God's love in all that he did. "When people meet me, I want them to see Jesus' reflection, not me, as if I had a mirror angled for them to see heaven ... to see Jesus," he said. "I don't believe God wants me out on the street corner, thumping my chest and beating people over the head. He just wants me to reflect His love within the church and within the HIV community. That is where Herb and Tamara's hearts are, too. It's amazing that we are in total agreement about the fact that many churches are bound by fear and are not showing love nor showing compassion to today's leper as Jesus did 2000 years ago," Mike explained.

HE INTENDS VICTORY

Mike was driving with Steve Willems, a friend and neighbor who had been the manager of Maranatha Village a huge Christian bookstore in Santa Ana, when the "He Intends Victory" name was born.

"Our hearts had been knit together," explained Mike. "I was HIV positive and Steve was dealing with the sale and closure of Maranatha Village. We were both going through difficult times. This was when I was extremely weak and needed somebody to talk to. I had not told Steve that I was HIV positive, but he was smart enough to know that my health was very bad," said Mike. "He never pried into what was going on in my life, but I know he and his wife, Joann, were praying for me. This was my first experience of telling someone that I was HIV positive," recalled Mike. "Steve responded by saying, 'I know. Joann and I have been praying for you for years.'" Steve and Mike continued to share their desire to be used by God, to be tuned in to hear the Word of God.

"One day, we were driving through our development here in Costa Mesa and trying to come up with a name for a ministry that I felt the Lord was calling me into," said Mike. "As we drove together, it was like the movie, *'Close Encounters of the Third Kind'* when suddenly, whoomph, a light hit the truck and Steve verbalized the words 'He Intends Victory'—HIV! We both got goose bumps as he said those words. It was as if the Lord were saying, 'I intend victory for AIDS and you have become one of My messengers.'"

A couple of months after coining this name, Mike became a founding board member of He Intends Victory supported in prayer and in many other ways by the Village Church of Irvine. He joined forces with people like Herb Hall, Tamara Brown and Bruce Sonnenberg.

Mike recalls speaking at an AIDS seminar at the Village Church of Irvine during the summer of 1992. Pastor Bruce Sonnenberg had written on the blackboard, "HIV, Human Immunodeficiency Virus."

Mike said, "When it was my turn to speak, I said, 'Bruce, that's wrong. Can I please change it?' I scratched out the world's definition of HIV and scribbled 'He Intends Victory.'"

Mike told the group that he felt that this is what God wanted to accomplish with this virus.

"I really think victory is what He wants to accomplish and victory is what He is wanting for Tamara, Herb, Bruce, and me," said Mike. "The victory is to bring the message to those that are entrenched in sin, for the people dying of AIDS to be shown the love of God, and for God to work in their lives." Mike said that He Intends Victory also wants to demonstrate to churches how to reach out to those with HIV and AIDS. "But before we and the churches can effectively minister to any group or individual, we must be on our knees in prayer asking for the Lord's will. It has been amazing to find people with that same calling, the same heart's desire. He Intends Victory is our gift from God which we're to use for His glory," Mike said.

INNOCENT VICTIM?

I wondered what Mike's response is to people who take the view that Herb and Tamara deserved to get the AIDS virus, but he was an innocent victim.

"There is an idea out there about innocent victims of this disease, and to me it's a distraction straight from the enemy," Mike stated. "I've been diagnosed with AIDS as have both Herb and Tamara. I also know hundreds of other people who are HIV positive.

"I acquired it through contaminated blood products. Herb and Tamara and others got it through a particular action or accident. Herb, Tamara, and I are not innocent victims. AIDS is a product of sin, not a judgment from God. We must stop categorizing one person's sin (i.e., homosexuality) and matching it to another's sin (i.e., lying) and then trying to determine a level of innocence. Let God judge the sinner and the sin. No one is 'an innocent victim' because **we all fall short of the glory of God.** We need to identify sin with the primary focus of restoring the sinner to God. Lying may or may not be as bad as homosexuality. Who's to judge? Sin is sin!

"I may not have been involved in a particular sin, but this virus, like disease itself, is a product of man's sin. I try to explain my concept regarding the term 'innocent victim' because within the hemophilia community you hear that a lot. I've heard others state that homosexuals and drug users are the non-innocent victims," Mike continued. "I know how I was infected with the AIDS virus, but regardless of how I was infected, I'm a sinful human being that God continues to love—somehow."

I wondered how Mike's children had responded to all of the setbacks.

"Well," said Sharon, "Our kids are now teenagers and at times may have had a certain amount of resentment when they found that Dad couldn't do something or we'd have to change plans in mid-stream. Never-the-less, it's something they've lived with all of their lives, and they have accepted the situation. Our kids are very special to us and I know they love their father. Courtney who is eighteen occasionally goes with Mike when he is speaking and has had a couple of opportunities to speak to church youth groups. She has a vast understanding of what the future holds for her generation if they choose to believe what the world is telling them and turn their backs on Scripture."

A MESSAGE TO THE CHURCH

Mike feels that the church is so much into politics, finger pointing, and the business of religion that it has allowed Satan "to keep us divided and distracted."

He added, "If the enemy can keep us divided, then we will not be on our knees seeking the Lord. We will spend our time fighting each other. It has become obvious to me that we are in a relentless spiritual battle. When we start praying constantly and seeking the leading of the Lord, that is when change will occur. Every Christian has a calling and we all need to be walking in the footprints of Jesus."

His message to the church is contained in Romans 12:9-12: *"Love must be sincere. Hate what is evil, cling to what is good, be devoted to one another in brotherly love. Honor one another above yourself. Never be lacking in zeal, but keep your spiritual fervor, serving the Lord. Be joyful in hope, patient in affliction, and faithful in prayer."*

Mike stated, "There are people dying of cancer, of alcoholism, and of hunger. We have all kinds of disease and sickness— HIV/AIDS is just one. However, HIV/AIDS is an epidemic that has the potential to wipe out the coming generation. The enemy is after our children, our future," Mike continued. "We must not allow this to continue. We must take a stand for God every day of the week—not just for a few hours on Sunday!

"Yes, I see AIDS as far more threatening than alcoholism or cancer. AIDS reflects how bad off we are spiritually, and the churches, especially the churches, have got to start loving, stop fighting, and stop being afraid. I wish I could get down on my knees, but I can't because of my illnesses. However, I truly believe that we need to start 'seriously' seeking the direction of the Lord. Each person, each church, has a ministry the Lord wants for them. All of the other things that divert us are distractions the enemy uses to keep us off balance.

"The church must put on the whole armor of God and reach out to people who are hurting. Many of the people who are hurting are HIV positive and dying in hospitals. I know the Lord is speaking to others saying, 'Go! Minister to people.' God is saying, 'Share with them who I am. Tell them I love them. No matter what they've done, I will forgive them. I sent My Son to die for all of you.'

"That will be a wonderful thing to see when people really start seeking God's direction. Why is our faith so weak and our work so ineffective?" Mike continued. "Christian apathy! Christian apathy is a symptom of not seeking God. We must return to the place where we knew God and where we had real zeal and an overwhelming desire to please Him.

"I'm not saying that we must all go out, stand on a corner and thump a Bible, preaching the end of the world. Still, we are to seek God's leading and if God leads you to go down to the beach and talk with the kids that are there skating and half naked, then that is where God wants you. If he wants you to set up an HIV ministry, then set up an HIV ministry."

Mike, being a computer programmer, said that when he has written a program, he has to make sure that all the little daggers that can attack it are covered. So one day Mike wrote down a list of priorities in his life. "God is number one," he said. He listed being a husband/father as priority two. He said family, health, home and financially providing for his family was number three and priority four was other family and friends. His church and "He Intends Victory" is a further priority.

"I look at my life only in the period that I can see which is right now and backwards," said Mike. "I cannot see ahead a minute from now, an hour, two days, or three, but I can step back and say,

'I'm going to try to look at myself from God's perspective.' That may sound strange but as God looks at me, I'm healed, physically. I'm healed! Whenever He sees Mike Hylton down here, I'm healed.

"Through my faith in Jesus Christ, I am physically healed! It may not be manifested until the moment I go to be with my Lord. That might happen two minutes from now. I continue to pray for healing for others and for myself. When God so chooses, we will be shown our healing."

I asked Sharon how she has handled her husband's many illnesses. "I don't know that it's really something that you handle, per se," she said. "It's more that I accept the circumstances. Realizing that we are in God's will shows us that God will provide and we just go on day-by-day, and try to stay focused on Him.

"We could drown in any situation if we let ourselves take some other perspective on it, but I think you have to really be honest. You have to have hope and faith. Some days Mike has good days, and then we do lots of things as a family. Those days are terrific." As Sharon smiled, she said, "On the bad days we just avoid him."

I asked Sharon what she would say to someone who has discovered they're HIV positive if they're in a church and are terrified to tell anybody.

"I think if they really feel that way, they're in the wrong place," she said. "They could contact 'He Intends Victory'. There are people in that ministry who understand and can help!"

The most loving church for the Hylton's has been a church 3,000 miles from their California home. "It's a small country church in Virginia where we attended for about nine months in 1988-1989. This was during a time when Mike's health was failing and we thought the East Coast area might be the best place to raise the kids in the long run. The church is called the College Park Church of Christ in Winchester, Virginia," she said.

"They are an extraordinary group of people, and we still get the church bulletin every Sunday. We know the prayer warriors in that church. We still get notes from people in the church and that is an encouragement. It's great. Their pastor, Larry Veach, has a heart of gold and has ministered to our family in many ways that only God could direct," Sharon said.

Mike says that he will never give up hope with his HIV condition. His T-cells have been down as low as sixty, but recently, after taking the d4T drug for a short time, his T-cells have risen to the mid 300's.

"That is a miracle in itself," he said. "I would say that is a tremendous jump."

He sees his ministry to "promote an awakening and an awareness of God the Father, God the Son, and God the Holy Spirit within the church and the HIV-infected community." He also wants to promote faith, hope and love of a living and personal God. As for Mike, he believes more than ever that "He Intends Victory" for people with AIDS.

Having talked to Herb about naming his T-cells, I asked Mike what he would name his last T-cell. I was not surprised when Mike responded without hesitation. He said, "HOPE!"

Mike later told me that he asked each of his children the same question, "If you had AIDS, what would you name your last T-cell?" Mike said he had to hold back tears as his thirteen-year-old son Todd replied, "I'd call mine DAVID. You know, Dad, David and Goliath."

Bruce Sonnenberg

and the Village Church

Chapter Thirteen

STAND BY ME

Bruce Sonnenberg was fighting back the tears as he stood before his congregation one Sunday morning with something heavy on his heart that he wanted to share with them. It was about a young man who had been asked to leave his church in Los Angeles after he had revealed to the pastor that he was HIV positive.

"We are a small congregation, but nonetheless, I need to know where you stand concerning people with AIDS," said Bruce, aware that he was about to ask his flock to do something that could split the church right down the middle. "I want to know if this church is going to be a place where all people can come, and that includes those who are HIV positive or have AIDS," Bruce continued.

Some in the congregation shuffled nervously in their seats and you could cut the atmosphere with a knife.

"There are many things we don't know about this disease," Bruce continued, "but it is also true that God loves these people and when they are hurting, they need somewhere they can come. If you agree with me and are willing to love people who are in this condition, please stand."

As perspiration beaded on the young pastor's forehead, there was a long, terrible silence. People brooded over the request and then one by one, they rose to their feet until everyone in the 260-member congregation was standing.

As he allowed his eyes to sweep those before him, Bruce Sonnenberg, his voice choking with emotion, said, "Thank you for showing the same compassion that Jesus did to the lepers of his time."

This incredible moment in time had solidified the church. Whatever other congregations in America decided, Bruce knew that, beyond a shadow of doubt, the Village Church of Irvine was going to stand up for those that were hurting.

"From that time forward, we were really united on this policy," he said.

THE UNLIKELY CANDIDATE

Bruce Sonnenberg is an unlikely man to be heading up a ministry that works with people who are HIV positive. Unlike Herb Hall and Tamara Lindley Brown, he's never been promiscuous. Contrary to Mike Hylton's experience, he does not have any life threatening illnesses.

He has lead a very ordinary life, but maybe that is why God has chosen him to bring stability and love into the lives of so many who had reached the end of their rope. He reaches out to those who have experienced rejection by their friends, their family and their churches.

On the road to becoming a pastor, Bruce studied for a year at a Bible school in San Antonio, Texas. "It was a very good school with wonderful people, but I quickly discovered that they had a totally different theology than mine," Bruce said. "I was Trinitarian and they were oneness, but I learned that they loved the same Jesus that I did."

In 1965, Bruce met Joni, an attractive young woman who attended the same church. The pair fell in love and they got married over Christmas in 1969.

Eventually, in May of the following year, the couple decided to return to California when school was over and Bruce continued his Bible training at Southern California College in Costa Mesa.

"While I was there, I got involved with Calvary Chapel of Costa Mesa and was in charge of the children's ministries—kindergarten through the eighth grade," recalled Bruce.

"Life became very hectic for me. Besides working full-time, I was overseeing the children's ministries at Calvary on Sunday mornings and Sunday nights and then Friday evenings I was responsible for the 'After Glow' of Ken Gulliksen's ministry." On top of all of this, the couple had three children as well.

"After two years, I graduated from Southern California College and Chuck Smith, senior pastor of Calvary Chapel, asked if I would oversee a new children's ministry," said Bruce. "The church was starting Maranatha Academy, but I really didn't feel called to do that. I knew that God had called me to be a pastor."

RIDING HIGH IN SKY VALLEY

Bruce, Joni and their family decided to visit Bruce's parents in Sky Valley near Palm Springs, California. "My parents had started a ministry there five years earlier called Sky Valley Desert Retreat," said Bruce. "There was a little church there that had sprung from that ministry. They didn't have a pastor and so they eventually called me to take up that position in 1972. In September, we all moved from Costa Mesa to the desert and lived there for ten years."

In October 1972, Bruce started "Changes", a radio ministry, and he has been on the radio weekly ever since.

"The church in Sky Valley grew and we had a wonderful time," said Bruce. "However, in 1982, the Lord put it on my heart to move to Irvine and establish the Village Church. We did just that and it was quite an exciting time in our lives. It was a real step of faith." Irvine was then a fast-growing, bedroom community in Orange County which, unlike most of the other towns in the area, had very few churches.

"That was one of the things I really looked into," said Bruce. "I didn't want to move into a town that already had too many churches. I didn't want to compete. We linked with a couple from Irvine that we initially met when they lived in the desert. The wife had met the Lord at Sky Valley and so Joanie and I got together with them. We asked them how they felt about us moving to Irvine and being a part of their community.

"They got really excited and began to pray with us about it. Irvine was a neighborhood of about 50,000 people at the time. We saw that it was a growing community and would probably double if not triple in size. There was a village community to each part of the city and so the Lord gave us the name—the Village Church of Irvine."

At the time, there were only about twenty churches in Irvine. "Now there are only about thirty," said Bruce, "which is still relatively few on a percentage per capita basis for a population that has now grown to 120,000."

After starting the Village Church of Irvine, as was his custom, Bruce became deeply involved in the local community.

"I helped start an organization called Irvine Temporary Housing which is now a very large community service organization helping homeless people," he explained. "I was on their board for three years."

Bruce also joined the board of the Orange County Rescue Mission in 1982 when he moved to Irvine. "I was chairman for two of those years, and resigned in 1992," he said. "I also have been involved with other ministries and organizations over the years as well, but pastoring is where my heart is. I love doing that. I have a wonderful congregation here."

For the first four years of the church, the main problems that Bruce had to cope with were couples separating and other families who were dealing with unruly offspring. But in 1986, without even realizing it, he first became involved with the AIDS epidemic.

"A lovely couple in our congregation who were active within the church, came to see me in my office," Bruce remembers. "They had been Roman Catholics and had been baptized in the Holy Spirit. They wanted me to meet their son of whom they were extremely proud. He was living up in L.A. on his own and they wanted me to pray for him.

"So I met him on a couple of occasions at the church office. Shortly after that, he made an appointment to see me and shared with me that he had been in the homosexual lifestyle and had lived with a man who had just died of AIDS. He had also been using and selling drugs."

With tears in his eyes, the young man confessed, "I've been tested and I am HIV positive. I don't know how to break it to my parents." Bruce told him that he just needed "to tell them the truth".

"He did just that and the news devastated them," said Bruce. "They not only found that their son was HIV positive, but also that he was living in a lifestyle that they felt was wrong."

Fortunately, they stood by him. "His parents loved him very much and I started meeting with him about once a week for three or four months," said Bruce. "At each get-together I would tell him about the love of Jesus for him. One day, he received the Lord as his personal Savior, and some very good things began to happen in his life. A year after that, his dad died very suddenly. It was a very hard time in their lives."

The young man had started going to "Faith Church" because there was a group of ex-homosexuals meeting there. "He opened my heart to those who are HIV positive," explained Bruce. "I could see that he needed someone to minister to him and someone to love and not condemn him. He had confessed his sin to the Lord and was struggling through all that, but nonetheless we, as a church, needed to stand with him.

"So, although he left our congregation, his parents stayed and when his father died, his mother started worshipping with him. During the time that I had been counseling him, he talked about a friend who was going to church in Los Angeles. He had started getting involved with that church. Thinking he could trust the pastor, he shared with him that he was HIV positive. When the pastor found that out, he told him that he was no longer welcome to come to church. It was too dangerous—he should stay away."

When Bruce heard this story, he was infuriated. It was then that he asked his congregation to stand with him to make sure this never happened at the Village Church of Irvine.

Chapter Fourteen

CAN YOU HEAR ME?

"I now pronounce you husband and wife," said Pastor Bruce on August 8, 1986, at the conclusion of a beautiful outdoor wedding ceremony. It had taken place amid blooming flowers and to the inspiring background of bird-song.

With that Kurt turned and kissed his new bride and their wonderful new life together began—or so it seemed to all that had witnessed this happy occasion! Tragically, however, the joy for this couple was to be short-lived.

Bruce had first met Kurt sometime before the congregation's "vote of confidence" in his AIDS policy.

"Kurt was a heroin addict who had come to church one Sunday," explained Bruce. "On that occasion, a man in our gathering who had been a drug user, shared his testimony and through that, Kurt gave his life to the Lord.

"It was wonderful to see such a change in his life. He lived in L.A. and really started growing in the Lord. After about a year, Kurt called me and said he wanted to get married. He had met a Christian woman and wondered if I would perform the wedding ceremony. He said he wanted the ceremony to take place in Orange County at his sister's home."

So Pastor Sonnenberg, amid the greenery of the garden, married the happy couple. "It was a delightful occasion and everything seemed to be well with this much-in-love couple," said Bruce.

About a year after that, Bruce got a disturbing call from Kurt's sister. "My brother's in the hospital with AIDS," she shared anxiously over the phone. "It has been a terrible blow," she sighed resignedly.

"What happened?" Bruce asked, astonished with the terrible news.

The woman explained that Kurt had received a call about the time he was to get married, from an old girlfriend, who had told him, "Kurt, I want you to know that I've got AIDS and you need to be tested."

Bruce continued, "She told me that Kurt went into denial. He didn't want to be tested. He didn't want to accept it. But he had gotten real sick, so he finally took the test. They discovered that the AIDS was very advanced. Kurt was so ill that the hospital admitted him then and there."

Bruce went to visit Kurt, but was not prepared for what he was about to see. His jaw tightened as he saw Kurt. "They had him in an isolation booth," Bruce recalled. "There was glass all around it. He had an intravenous tube in his arm which had come out and there was blood all over his arm and on his bed. It was terrible.

"Kurt was strapped down and was in convulsions. He was unable to talk," said Bruce. He could only sit on the side of the bloody bed and look into Kurt's blue, distressed face that showed his complete exhaustion.

"Kurt, this is Bruce," he said softly as he looked desperately into the bloodshot slits that passed for Kurt's eyes. Bruce didn't know whether Kurt was cognizant or not.

"Do you remember who I am?" he asked. "If you do, blink your eyes."

As life was ebbing out of his wasted body, Kurt was able to do just that, so the pastor knew he was aware of what was being said.

"Kurt, I haven't seen you for the last year. I don't know where you've been or how you're doing, but are you walking with Jesus?" Bruce asked. Kurt fluttered his lids again as Bruce noticed that Kurt's face had an alarming bluish cast with deep maroon colored lips. Then Bruce said, "Are you ready to go be with the Lord?"

About that time, the nurse came in and noticed that Bruce wasn't wearing a mask, gown or gloves. She scooted him out and made him don all of the protective paraphernalia before letting him back into the booth. Again Bruce asked, "Kurt, are you ready to go to be with the Lord?" Kurt's eyes acknowledged that he was. "So I prayed with him," said Bruce as Kurt's chest was heaving violently. "It was excruciating to watch." The next day, Kurt's short uneven breath stopped and he passed into eternity. Bruce was asked to perform the funeral ceremony.

By now, his wife had been tested and she was also found to be HIV positive. "Naturally, she was heartbroken and confused," stated Bruce. "She wouldn't even come to the funeral. So in June of 1988, we did a memorial service here at the church and his close family members attended. It was a touching time, but through it, my heart had become aware of the terrible predicament of those who are HIV positive. I ended up being sensitive to the illness and reading as much information as I could about it."

THE AIDS EPIDEMIC

Bruce read in one newspaper report that about one-fifth of those living in the streets of America had the AIDS virus. This really began to concern him.

"Being the chairman of the board of the Orange County Rescue Mission, I was close to the men living there," he said. "We always insisted that they had to go to a church and a lot of them liked to come here which we enjoyed. Two of the men who were in the 'New Life Program' graduated to become staff members at the Rescue Mission. Both men were HIV positive, so now we had two such people in our congregation. I began talking with John Wilson, one of them, one day and we discussed how important it was for the people to have a support group. I realized that those who are HIV positive need to have a place where they can talk and open up their hearts."

So Bruce Sonnenberg worked it out with the director of the rescue mission to give the HIV-infected men the liberty to attend a Tuesday night meeting which began in September, 1990. There were surprising side effects to Bruce's open attitude at the church. "Since we started this support group, one of our elders and another leader in the church, discovered that both of their brothers who were homosexuals, had contacted AIDS. The brothers have since died," explained Bruce. "We prayed for them as a congregation and our elders both witnessed the Lord at work in the lives of their brothers. So the group became even more supportive of people in the church."

This cross-fertilization has brought a tremendous love into the church. "When the street people first started coming, the family members of the church would talk to them and ask them how they were feeling. It grew to be, 'Oh, you're my brother now.' They also reached out to those who were in church and were going through this ordeal."

The church started announcing the HIV-positive support group on the radio as well as in the local newspaper.

"We always start our week with a word of prayer," said Bruce. "I decided that the support group would be open to anybody, but it was not going to be a time for medical discussion. The spiritual was to be most important. Still, we always opened the week by asking people how their T-cell count was. The reason was that it was a way for them to identify with each other."

He said that when somebody was 400, they would all be encouraged, but if one of the group was down to around 20, Bruce would say, "Well, praise the Lord. Let's pray for you."

"HOW'S YOUR T-CELLS?"

Bruce Sonnenberg said they all knew it was more discouraging if the person's T-cells were generally down to those lower numbers. "Most healthy people have a T-4 cell count of 800 to 1,200, so we always look to a 1,000 as the average," he explained. "This is the number of white cells, or T-4 cells per one million red blood cells. Those are the cells that fight infection. Those are the immunity cells. The virus attacks those cells first. When somebody gets this virus in their blood, it immediately attacks those cells and begins to destroy them."

Bruce soon discovered that when that process begins, a person's T-cell count starts to go down. "When someone gets to 200 and below, they are diagnosed with AIDS, also known as 'full-blown AIDS,'" he explained. "If their T-cell count is above 200 without having an opportunistic infection, they are generally described as being HIV positive."

One of the blessings of the support groups has been that they have always been small. "We generally have about four people at a time," he said. "Mostly, we get men, but there have also been several women who have come once or twice over the years."

Bruce says his heart has really gone out to women who learn they are HIV positive. "I remember one woman in particular who was a high school leader at her church," said Bruce. "She had a one night fling with a guy from the church years earlier and he left and moved away. Then she had found out that he had infected her with this virus and she was afraid to tell her pastor. Also, she was afraid to tell anybody in the church because she believed she would be asked to leave.

"When we heard her sad story, everybody in the group started ministering to her," recalled Bruce. "She didn't know when or how to tell anybody about her predicament. One of our group said, 'Hey, the Lord will show you when and how to tell people.' That is how the group started ministering.

"We also looked for a way to serve the Lord with this ministry. We had people who would come for a while and then move on. Prayerfully we have shared our ministry with these individuals as well."

A CALL TO CASEY

Bruce remembers Casey, who had received the Lord into his heart and was involved with a church in Huntington Beach. "Then he got really sick and could no longer attend," said Bruce. "We all sat in the church office and I put the speaker phone on and talked with him and prayed for him. The next night he died. It was such a blessing to be able to gather like this. It took the focus off the individual and put it on the other person. That was very healthy."

Andrew Johnson was another regular in the support group. "He was a fine fellow," said Bruce. "He was working two full-time jobs despite being HIV positive. Andrew was initially strong and healthy and started getting weaker and weaker and eventually he couldn't come anymore. He was a dynamic young man who's since gone to be with the Lord."

Bruce says the hardest thing about the AIDS ministry is knowing that the people that he works with and loves are probably going to die soon. "That is the most difficult thing because I love them."

I asked Bruce what he perceived to be the overall attitude of the church today toward people who are HIV positive or have AIDS. "Ignorance. That's the general attitude," he said. "Because of this, there is also fear which causes people to keep their distance from people with this problem. They are afraid that their children will somehow contract the disease by being in the same room as those with the AIDS virus. In view of all of this misunderstanding, we at He Intends Victory are developing church policies, trying to help alleviate some of those fears for churches."

I wondered what he felt would be Jesus' attitude toward the HIV-positive community today.

"The comparison about Jesus and the leper is that He touched the leper," Bruce said. "I went to a debate on the topic of AIDS recently and a woman stood up and said that Jesus touched the leper after He healed him. My personal response to her statement was that Jesus touched the leper before he was healed. He didn't heal him and then touch him. He touched the leper first. The Lord didn't say, 'Well, this might be a risk to my ministry.' He just loved him.

"I think there is a place where caution comes in, but also we need to step over that boundary and trust the Lord, too. But I think that generally we need to respond out of real love and direction. We need to love that person."

He added, "The other side of this disease is that AIDS is an Acquired Immune Deficiency, meaning that people have acquired it. They've gotten it by doing something. Ninety-eight percent of the people who have this disease, acquired it because they've done something that is wrong. Now, I can't look down on them too long," he went on, "because I'm sinful myself. It's only by grace that I'm saved. So we don't want to condemn anyone, but we know that by and large, the mode of transmission of this disease has been through the homosexual and bisexual community. Even among homosexuals, if they had just stayed monogamous, they probably wouldn't have contacted this disease."

Bruce says that in view of this, the Christian church needs to speak out and say, "There is a consequence for sin, but at the same time, if you have this disease, we want you to know that we love you because we are saved by grace, too."

I asked the pastor why it appeared that the Christian church had singled out homosexuality as "the worst sin" anyone could commit. He said, "I think there are two reasons for that. One is that it is called an abomination in the Scripture so it is looked upon as a heavier type sin. I do believe that there are different consequences for different sins. In the Old Testament if you said something against someone that was sinful, there was a consequence for it. If you stole, there was a different consequence, but if you murdered, there was a more severe consequence. However, forgiven sin is all the same."

He said, "Since the King James version of the Bible describes homosexuality as an abomination, people are inclined to look down upon homosexuals with disdain. That is sad because it tends to make us feel righteous because we haven't done such a "bad" sin. That's not the idea at all. The truth is that we are all sinners saved by grace."

Bruce Sonnenberg does not described the HIV virus as God's punishment for the homosexual community. "If that were so, what is cancer?" he asked. "Is breast cancer, for instance, God's way of punishing women? Is prostate cancer God's way of punishing men? Of course not! God doesn't work that way. Sickness is a consequence for all of us living in a sinful world."

He said his plea to the church today is, "Open your heart to those with the HIV virus. Jesus has given us a new heart and it has lots of room in it for the hurting, for those in pain and for those in need. We, in the church, are those called by the Lord to reach out with a tender heart and tell them that Jesus loves them and forgives them. In fact, God intends victory for all of us"!

Chapter Fifteen

HIGHWAY TO HEAVEN

When Jim and Ellie Johnston, both originally from Belfast, Northern Ireland, first learned that their youngest son, Andrew, was homosexual, they thought he was on a highway to hell. But, as he passed into eternity on November 17, 1992, at 2:55 P.M., they knew for a fact that he was, instead, on a beautiful highway to heaven. The couple agreed to talk about their moving experience with Tim Berends, radio co-host on the "Tim and Al Show" on KBRT-AM radio in Costa Mesa, California. Tim is also a board member of the He Intends Victory ministry. The Johnston s spoke about their incredible experience shortly after losing their thirty-five-year-old son to AIDS.

"We were devastated when he first came home and told us that he was homosexual," said Ellie.

Jim said he asked himself, "What did I do wrong and what can we do now to bring him back into the path of the Lord?"

Jim revealed that it was the Holy Spirit and the Lord Jesus that won Andrew back. "He loved all the beautiful hymns of the church," he recalled. "He loved the Lord, and the last year of his life was a beautiful, tender walk with Jesus. He truly wanted to go home to be with the Lord."

Andrew had been out of the homosexual lifestyle for five years when he passed away. The couple discovered that their son had AIDS after he came down with pneumonia in October of 1988.

"He just kept deteriorating from there on," remembered Jim Johnston.

Anne Laudadio, Andrew's sister, explained that several pastors whom Andrew loved dearly came to see him and to comfort our family prior to his passing. One of them was Chuck Smith, senior pastor of Calvary Chapel of Costa Mesa.

"He spoke some encouraging words to Andrew and then Dad asked Pastor Chuck if he would sing, 'Until Then My Heart Will Go On Singing,'" recalled Anne. "Pastor Chuck sang it beautifully, and Andrew and our entire family joined in. This was very remarkable since for the last year Andrew had not been able to sing because AIDS-related cancer was in his esophagus.

"The nurses said it sounded like angels were in Andrew's room and we all knew there were! We sang several more songs that were dear to Andrew. Andrew was exuberant and said he couldn't imagine a more joyous celebration than this. It brings such comfort when we think about the heavenly look on his face at that moment."

Anne went on to say, "After several hours, Andrew began to grow tired, and he closed his eyes. This was hard for us because we believed that once he went to sleep, we would not be able to speak with him again. There were tears, but the joy we experienced earlier that day had left us a with warm, wonderful feeling because we knew Andrew would not have to suffer much longer. Since our family had not slept or eaten for three days, with much coaxing, we all left Andrew's room together to get something to eat. We knew we might have a long vigil at Andrew's bedside until he took his last breath.

"A short time later, upon returning to Andrew's bedside, we were absolutely astonished to find Andrew awake and sitting up! The joy we felt at having one more time to tell Andrew we loved him, and talk to him was indescribable. We jumped up and down and laughed and cried and hugged each other.

"Andrew told us he had just been tired, and was sleeping, but he heard us all crying prior to leaving the room. He scolded us, and said he didn't want us to cry over him when he really did go. His doctor came into the room while all this rejoicing was going on and Andrew told him, 'I'm back.' Then talking about the morphine that had been administered to him to deal with the pain he was in, he added with his typical humor, 'This doesn't work! Where's the guarantee? I want my money back!'

Anne said the doctor walked out of the room scratching his head, saying, "You people are weird!"

Jim went on to talk about an extraordinary dream that Andrew had a couple of hours later about a black limousine. "Andrew," he said, "told us, 'You are going to have to go through this again, and I don't want any broken hearts, because this is a happy day. This is my coronation. I'm going to be with Jesus today.'"

As they sat by his bed, their son began recalling his boyhood years. "This went on for most of the evening and after about four hours, he finally fell asleep again," said Jim.

He again woke up and began telling his family, "I see a black limousine with black windows."

The family listened intently as he appeared to be addressing someone in the limousine whom they surmised to be the devil. Andrew said in a firm voice, "You deceived me once, but you will never deceive me again."

His sister Anne who was beside his bed, leaned over and asked, "Andrew, where are you now? What are you seeing?"

Andrew's eyes lit up like a lamp as he remarked, "I'm in a beautiful green garden."

Anne continued her questioning. "Andrew, can you describe it to us?"

He replied, "I see a bright light up ahead. It is so bright, it is almost blinding. I need sunglasses, but then again, I never really liked sunglasses."

"Is it too beautiful to describe?" Anne then asked.

Andrew shook his head and replied, "No, but I am walking and I'm not feeling any pain." After a brief moment, he continued. "Now I'm sitting on a beautiful marble bench made of unhewn marble and it doesn't hurt me to sit on it."

Anne said, "He told us that he was able to walk again! He told us that he was able to see a lot of people, but he couldn't recognize anyone."

She asked him, "Can you see Jesus yet?"

He responded, "Not yet," a big smile crossing his face.

Anne recalled that her brother kept talking for a another eight hours. "The entire time, his eyes were closed, but he knew right where everyone in the room was seated," she said.

Jim Johnston stated that Andrew's conversation wasn't the "typical Andrew—it was a very college level conversation that we were having with him, almost like a message from above."

Anne asked again, "Where are you now?"

Andrew replied, "I see the gates just up ahead. They are beautiful and made of suspended, uncut pearls." He described each gate as being one giant pearl.

He added, "They go on as high and wide as you can see."

As he stood before the pearly gates of heaven, Andrew declared, "Now that I'm here, I need a verse—First Corinthians 6." Andrew's eyes were happily peering into the next world.

Jim Johnston got out his Bible and began reading verses 19 and 20, "*Do you not know that your body is the temple of the Holy Spirit, who is in you, whom you have from God.*" When he got to verse 20, "*You are not your own, You are bought with a price, the precious blood of Jesus,*" Andrew quoted every word with his father.

"It was delightful," recalled Jim, "just like he was reading it himself."

Andrew then said, "I'm going in, but I need a song."

So, tearfully, Jim Johnston began singing "There's a Highway To Heaven," as everyone joined in.

"That's my song!" he declared joyfully. Andrew joined in the singing. After the song was over, Andrew said, "I'm walking through the gates, and now that I'm inside, I realize that you don't need any passes or credentials here."

Jim Johnston explained that when Andrew had gone into his sister's complex, he always had to have a pass at the gate.

"There are no passes here and you don't need any papers," said Andrew, his face flushed with heavenly joy.

Jim said that after his son had gone inside, he said, "I'm looking back in the direction of the gates, and I can see the words, 'You made the right choice.'"

Andrew added, "Isn't this strange? I came to the Lord when I was a little boy, but now that I'm here, I find God saying, '*You have not chosen me but I have chosen You.*'" With that, Andrew Johnston passed into the presence of his Lord. As Andrew closed his eyes for the last time and drew his last breath at 2:55 P.M., Jim turned to his daughter and said, "You know, some of the years were rough and the last one has really been a trial, but Andrew passed over to the other side like a saint."

After the family came away from the bedside, Jim wondered aloud, "Why aren't we crying? Why aren't we completely destroyed?"

He later understood, "It was because he had left us with word from the other side that he had arrived. He was happy to be in his eternal home."

Anne said, "The Lord gave our family such peace and comfort. It is truly a peace that passes all understanding. We miss Andrew terribly, and grieve for ourselves at how much we miss him. We do not grieve for Andrew for he is with his Lord. He is no longer suffering."   Andrew Johnston had finally gone home to his wonderful reward and the Johnston family was at peace. One day, they will all be together again on the highway to heaven.

At her brother's funeral on November 2 at Florence Avenue Foursquare Church in Santa Fe Springs, California, Anne told the congregation, "Andrew told me how disappointed he was that he would not be able to attend today because he didn't want to miss out, but he had another engagement booked for today. He was the guest of honor at a welcome home celebration.... My father said he died like a saint, and he did."

Welcome home, Andrew!

BROTHERS IN ARMS

Greg Done's story of the last days of his brother Tony's life was equally moving, but there was a completely different twist to this story. Speaking before the congregation of the Village Church of Irvine, he explained about Tony's last days on earth. He also died of AIDS complications.

Greg's voice was strangely hushed and nervous as he began by sharing a couple of the Scriptures. The first was from Romans 10, verses 9 and 10, in which the Apostle Paul said, "*If we confess with our mouth Jesus Christ as Lord and believe in our hearts that God raised him from the dead, you will be saved."* He added, *"If we confess our sins, he is faithful and just to forgive us our sins and to cleanse us from all unrighteousness."*

Greg revealed that his brother, who was gay, was diagnosed as having AIDS in January, 1991.

"By December of 1991, he had deteriorated significantly," said Greg. "My brother and I had a relationship in which I was able to share the gospel with him several times. However, because of the gay community's perception that all Christians hate people with AIDS and that God's punishment is on people in the gay community, he had no perception of God's love at all."

Greg said that from January to September, 1992, God opened the door for his family to be able to spend some "quality time" with his brother. He said that if his daughter Tammy had been able to share with the church, she would say, "Love them. Care for them. Don't run from them."

Greg said that one day he was with his brother. "He was in bed and I crawled in beside him. We spent three or four hours together," he said as he burst into tears, recalling the incident. When he was able to recover his composure, he went on. "God's anointing was there and I was able to minister to my brother in a big way. When I left, I was floating out of the room. He had received the gospel and it appeared to be good news to him."

Greg asked his brother, "Would you like to have more?" He responded by nodding his head in the affirmative. "Yes, come back. I want more."

Greg's heart leapt with excitement. The next week, Greg called his brother at the hospital, and said, "I'm ready to come back."

He was shocked when his brother responded with deep bitterness in his voice, "Don't bother," he snapped. "You can be my brother, but that God stuff has to go. I'm sick of it! I don't want to hear any more about it. Stay away!" Tony paused briefly and then added, "If you want to come as my brother, fine, but I don't want any more of that God baloney."

Greg confessed to feeling extremely dismayed with this turn of events. "I was shocked because it seemed like God had done such a work there, so I called up my pastor, Bruce Sonnenberg, and a good friend of mine, Dr. Eno. I asked, 'What do I do? I can't say anything right now. I'm just going to go back. I'm just going to open that door again,'" he recalled.

"Dr. Eno said to me, 'Don't do that. God loves him more than you do. Pray for a door of opening and just be available and ready. Let's see what God will do.'"

Members of the family sat with him. "My wife, Marie, spent several days during which she would scratch his back, rub his feet and back, and change his diapers, but there was no spiritual response from him," said Greg.

Tony became so discouraged in August, 1992, that he decided he would go off of his $20,000-a-month drugs and "just die." Greg said, "I wanted to knock down the doors again, but I remembered the advice, 'Don't knock it down. God loves him more than you.' So I didn't. Eventually, God opened the door, and again we had a special time together of prayer. I was able to share God's word with my dying brother. He was open because he knew that he was opening the door between where he was and where he was going to spend all of eternity. He was dealing with that."

Greg said that several weeks later, after going on a camping trip, he and Marie heard the news that Tony had passed away. Marie told the Lord, "God, we needed just a little bit more time. Why did this happen before he accepted Jesus as his Savior?"

Greg was surprised to receive a phone call one day from his brother's homosexual lover asking him to conduct the memorial service.

"We went to the memorial service and I presided over it. People shared their memories of my brother," he recalled. "When it was just about over, a big black man who was my brother's nurse during the five weeks before he died said, 'I'd like to share something.' He was aglow, just like an angel," recalled Greg. "He said, 'As a nurse, I can't push my faith, but if a patient appears to be open to the Gospel, I can share it with them.'"

By now, Greg, and other people in the church began to weep, but the huge nurse pressed on with his incredible story.

"One day, Tony had an extremely bad day, and he said to me, 'I don't know where I'm going. I'm not sure.'"

The black nurse responded by asking the dying man, "Do you mind if I share some things with you from the Bible?"

"That's what I want," said Tony.

The nurse opened up his Bible and told Tony about God's wonderful plan of salvation. He asked him, "Do you believe that you've been in sin, that you are a sinner and the only way out is through Jesus Christ?"

Tony nodded his head and replied, "I believe that. I want to be forgiven. I want to turn my life over to Jesus. I want to spend all of eternity with Him."

The nurse with kindly sparkling eyes went on to reveal that Tony began to pray, "God, please forgive me for my sins. Please be my Lord."

The nurse said that Tony was open to all that he was able to tell him about his new life as a Christian after that. "They shared a lot," said Greg. "This big black preacher was a lay minister that God had placed in Tony's ward for that specific time."

The nurse concluded his speech by looking straight at Greg and the rest of the congregation. He said in a husky bass voice, "Don't you be worrying about Tony. Tony's okay. Instead, you should be worrying about yourself. Have you come to the place Tony came? Have you believed on Jesus Christ? If you haven't, you haven't come to the place that Tony did. So don't you be worrying about Tony," he added. "You be worrying about yourself."

There was a profound stillness in the congregation, then spontaneous applause broke out.

"It was so great to hear this news," said Greg. "My wife's heart just about burst with joy because she had said, 'God, you took him too soon, we needed a little bit more time.' God was saying to all of us, **'I'm always, always on time.'**"

Recalling joy of last moments

My dear brother Andrew,
You left our presence for a time, and entered into eternal life. The joy our family experienced with you in those last moments is something we will cherish the rest of our lives.

You were able to describe to us what you were seeing. You told us about the pearly gates that were open, and the light so bright that it was almost blinding. You described the beautiful garden you were in and said you were sitting on a marble bench and were walking again!

LIFE LETTERS

I will always love you, and you will hold a place in my heart that no one else can hold. I am thankful for the time God allowed us to be together. You are in a far better place than we can imagine, and you are no longer suffering.

"I will meet you in the morning."

(Andrew Johnston, 35, of San Clemente died Nov. 17.)

— **Anne Laudadio**
Santa Ana

Chapter Sixteen

AN AIDS POLICY FOR THE CHURCH

You have read the challenging stories of Herb Hall, Tamara Lindley Brown and Mike Hylton, as well as Jonathan and other victims who have endured crushing rejection from some of their peers because they suffer from the dreaded disease AIDS.

You have also read about others like Bruce Sonnenberg who have welcomed them into the warmth of a fellowship like the Village Church of Irvine. They have welcomed them with open and non-judgmental arms. They have followed the example of Jesus by reaching out and touching the modern-day lepers.

MODERN-DAY FALLACIES ABOUT AIDS

One of the problems is that there are so many stories floating around concerning how people contract the AIDS virus known as HIV. There are those that believe it can be transmitted through handshakes, hugs, toilet seats or doorknobs.

These fallacies go against modern-day scientific research. Scientists have done extensive studies to determine whether the virus can be transmitted in normal social gatherings. Definitive information shows that this cannot readily occur. The only documented cases of transmission outside the three primary modes have been of healthcare workers exposed to infected blood or body fluids. In these healthcare workers, infected blood or body fluids were either ingested or spilled on skin with cuts or abrasions. Although this risk is very low, it should alert healthcare workers to the dangers of transmission in the workplace either in the hospital or other healthcare settings. It should also inform others who do not have similar exposure, that the risk of exposure to this virus is minimal outside the three primary modes of transmission.

GUIDELINES FOR VISITING A FRIEND WITH HIV

When someone you know finds out they are HIV positive or have AIDS, you may feel inadequate to help. At this crisis moment in their life, they NEED YOU more than ever. If they are a friend, tell them to be sure to call you for anything even though out of fear and insecurity, you may feel apprehensive and inadequate when the call for help comes.

Here are some guidelines and suggestions on how to help someone who is HIV positive or has AIDS. This list has been provided by Love and Action Ministries:

*Try not to avoid your acquaintance. Be there because it instills hope. Be the friend, the loved one, you have always been, especially now when it is most important.

*Touch your friend. A simple squeeze of the hand or a hug can let him or her know that you care. (You need not be afraid— you cannot contract AIDS simply by touching. Hugs are very reassuring.)

*Call and ask if it is okay to come for a visit. Let your friend make the decision. He or she may not feel up to a visit that day. You can always visit on another occasion. Now is a time when your friendship can help keep loneliness and fear at a distance.

*Respond to your friend's emotions. Weep with your friend when he weeps. Laugh when he laughs. It is healthy to share these intimate experiences. They enrich you both.

*Don't be afraid to share the joy of knowing Jesus with your friend, but don't be overbearing. Don't demand immediate spiritual maturity, and full understanding. Remember you didn't get where you are in a second. On some occasions, the best witness is a simple prayer or a kindness shown (James 2:14-17).

*Be knowledgeable of God's power to heal even in the most difficult circumstances. It's okay, when praying with your friend, to give him hope by asking God to manifest His healing power. However, don't make your friend feel guilty if healing does not take place. Know that God may have other plans for your friend.

*Call and say you would like to bring a favorite dish. Ask what time and day would be best for you to visit. Spend time sharing a meal.

*Go for a walk or outing, but ask about and know your friend's limitations.

*Offer to help answer any correspondence which may be giving some difficulty or which your friend may be avoiding.

*Call your friend and find out if anything is needed from the store. Ask for a shopping list and make a delivery to your friend's house.

*Celebrate holidays and life with your friend by offering to decorate the home or hospital room. Bring flowers or special treasures. Include your friend in your holiday festivities. A holiday doesn't have to be marked on a calendar, you can make every day a holiday.

*When possible, stay in contact with your friend's family, roommate or care-partner. They may need a break from time to time. Offer to care for the person with AIDS in order to give their loved ones some free time. Invite them out.

* Your friend may be a parent. Ask about the children. Offer to bring them to visit.

*Be creative. Bring books, periodicals, taped music, a poster for the wall, home-baked cookies or delicacies to share.

*It's okay to ask about the illness, but be sensitive to whether or not your friend wants to discuss it. You can find out by asking, "Would you like to talk about how you are feeling?" However, don't exert pressure.

*Like everyone else, a person with AIDS can have both good and bad days. On the bad days, however, treat your friend with extra care and compassion.

*Can you take your friend somewhere? Transportation may be needed to a treatment, to the store, or to the bank, the physician, church, shopping or a movie. How about just a ride to the beach or a park?

*Ask your friend to make decisions. Illness can cause a loss of control over many aspects of life. Allow your friend the chance to make decisions, no matter how simple or insignificant they may seem to you.

*Be prepared for your friend to get angry with you for "no reason," although it seems you have been there and done everything you could. Remember anger and frustration are often taken out on people most loved because it is safe and will be understood.

*Outside information can be healthy. Keep your friend up-to-date on mutual friends and other common interests. Your friend may be tired of talking about symptoms, doctors and treatments.

*What's new in the news? Discuss current events. Help keep your friend from feeling that the world is passing him by.

*Offer to do household chores, perhaps doing the laundry, washing dishes, watering plants, feeding and walking pets. This may be appreciated more than you realize. However, don't do what your friend can do and wants to do for himself. Ask before doing anything.

*Don't lecture or direct anger at your friend if he seems to be handling the illness in a way that you think is inappropriate. You may not understand what the feelings are and why certain choices are being made.

*If you sense your friend is experiencing feelings of guilt or blame regarding the illness, remind that person that God is gracious, merciful and forgiving.

*A loving family member can be a source of strength. Remember that by being a friend you are also a part of the family.

*Do not confuse acceptance of the illness with defeat. Sometimes acceptance may free your friend to accept God's better plan for his or her life.

*Don't allow your friend, his family or roommate to become isolated. Let them know about support and prayer groups, Bible studies and other concrete practical services offered by your ministry, churches and agencies.

*Talk about the future with your friend...tomorrow, next week, next year. It is good to look toward the future without denying the reality of today.

*Take good care yourself. Recognize your own limitations and honor them. Share with your pastor and Christian friends your own feelings of grief, helplessness and inadequacy. Getting the emotional and spiritual support you need will help you to be there for the person who has AIDS.

IS YOUR CHURCH WILLING TO HELP?

If your church is willing to get involved and show Christ's love to HIV-positive and AIDS people and their families, He Intends Victory suggests that your church draw up a document similar to the following:

[— Our Church —] will welcome HIV positive (Human Immunodeficiency Virus) and AIDS (Acquired Immune Deficiency Syndrome) sufferers and their families with love and acceptance. The Christian response to a person with HIV/AIDS must be compassionate, helpful, and redemptive. Jesus, as our example, cared for those with disease with a personal demonstration of God's love.

Therefore, we the people of [— Our Church —] stand together in the following statement:

*We do not believe that those who have tested HIV positive or those who have AIDS have incurred a direct punishment from God.

*An HIV positive or AIDS person will not be excluded from the life of [— Our Church —].

*We encourage those who have AIDS or have tested HIV positive to make a confidential disclosure to a member of our church leadership so that we might assist in expressing God's love.

*Since the AIDS virus is not spread by casual contact, there should be no risk of contracting the AIDS virus from any infected adult or child in the church setting as long as no blood-to-blood contact takes place.

*AIDS is preventable! It can be prevented by avoiding sexual contact before marriage and by maintaining a faithful, monogamous, heterosexual relationship with an uninfected person in marriage for life. It can be prevented by avoiding illicit drug use.

*We commit ourselves to educating and teaching God's values. "*A new command I give you: Love one another as I have loved you, so you must love one another. All men will know that you are my disciples if you love one another.*" John 13:34,35

Chapter Seventeen

PERSONAL MESSAGES

A MESSAGE FROM HERB HALL

My heart and gratitude go out to my friend Dan Wooding who approached us to write this book. It was incredible how I met Dan about a year ago. Dan saw an article in the Southern California Christian Times about our AIDS ministry. He called me one day and introduced himself. During our conversation, Dan asked, "Herb, I have a friend who is a missionary to Uganda. He is an older man and has been in Uganda for years. This missionary has a vision in his heart to build a hospice in Uganda."

Dan told me that thirty to forty percent of Uganda's population is HIV positive and is expected to die of AIDS within the next three years. He asked if I would meet with his friend and be an encouragement to him. I visited this missionary friend and we shared our vision and desire to be used by God in AIDS ministries. I was very touched as he shared about the hospice and his AIDS ministry in Uganda.

After our meeting, I decided to locate Dan Wooding's office and meet this man with whom I had only talked on the phone. After meeting and talking with Dan, he said, "Herb, I'd like to do a story on your ministry." I jokingly asked him, "Who do you write for?" Dan responded, "Before I was a Christian I used to write for the tabloids and then when I became a Christian, God completely changed my heart and my writing goals."

What followed was an interview of Tamara and myself. As Dan heard our stories, I could see his heart and love for this particular ministry. The article Dan wrote and published was superb. With a heart for an AIDS ministry, we asked Dan to join the board of directors of He Intends Victory.

Some time later, Dan said to me, "Herb, you have an incredible testimony, how would you like to do a book?" I prayed and sought the Lord for direction. I thanked Dan for his offer and explained I did not feel in my heart that I was to become involved with a book project at this time.

With the vision still on Dan's heart, a few weeks later he again asked, "Herb, I know you did not want to participate in the book project with only your story, so how about doing a book on the entire He Intends Victory ministry? Three of the board members represent different ways you can be infected with this disease." I agreed that this was an excellent idea. Dan suggested that Pastor Bruce Sonnenberg of the Village Church of Irvine who had a passion to start an AIDS ministry and to develop an AIDS policy for churches also contribute to the book project.

This book came about because Dan Wooding had a vision! With my deepest and greatest gratitude, I thank my dear friend Dan Wooding for taking the time to interview us and write this book.

My gratitude to my family who, when I shared with them that I was HIV positive, reached out with love and compassion to me and accepted me. My family means the world to me and I'm very thankful for those who love me, stand by me and support me.

I also want to thank the people of my former church who continue to reach out and care for me, and my thanks to the people at my new church, the Village Church of Irvine, who have supported me and helped start this ministry.

I am thankful for the love and compassion that the Village Church of Irvine has given me and for all the new friends I have made these past few years through my involvement in AIDS ministries. My thankfulness goes out to the friends to whom I have had the opportunity to minister and who have given their

Personal Messages

lives to Jesus Christ. Some are now with the Lord having passed on because of this disease. My heart of caring goes out to the families that have lost their loved ones.

continmost important heartfelt message that I would like to leave my Lord and Savior Jesus Christ who has never left walks with me were never turned His back on me even though I His heart. I am thankful that my Lord

My heart is to share the gospel given me.
continues to change our lives and work the ministry of how God He can turn us from our sin. My hope for you is that you receive from this book, the message of Jesus Christ and the heart of Jesus Christ. I pray you take this message to other people who do not know Him and minister to them in their hurt and pain.

Again, I am grateful that we have had the opportunity to complete this book and thanks again to Dan Wooding and all of you.

God bless you,

Herb

A MESSAGE FROM MIKE HYLTON

What would Jesus do? Are HIV and AIDS a curse from God ... or opportunities from God? Please pray for the answer.

Please pray for our youth, who are the "high risk" group of today and tomorrow. Pray for behavioral changes, pray for our youth to make the right choices, to develop self respect, pride in themselves, commitment to what is right, and pray for values.

Please pray for spiritual awakening for the millions now dying of AIDS. Pray for spiritual awakening for the millions of

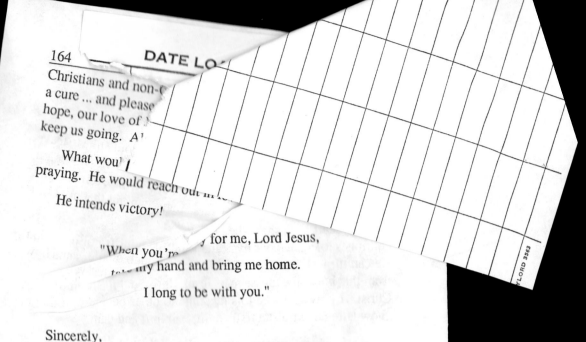

Christians and non-c...
a cure ... and please...
hope, our love of ...
keep us going. A...

What wou...
praying. He would reach out in...

He intends victory!

"When you're ... y for me, Lord Jesus,
... my hand and bring me home.

I long to be with you."

Sincerely,

Mike

A MESSAGE FROM TAMARA LINDLEY BROWN

To each individual who chose to read this book – thank you!

Being open and truthful is the best medicine that God has given me for HIV disease. I pray that as Christians, we will give all those infected – and affected – by HIV the same opportunity to be honest about the disease. I pray this will lead them to return to the unconditional, everlasting embrace of the Lord Jesus Christ to find the same love and peace that I have found.

With Love,

Tamara